T0053879

"I've read a lot of academic books during getting my degrees, and may pale into insignificance when compared with these books. But then I'm an Aboriginal woman Elder and I am biased. However, when you say that many in academia and the Australian government find it hard to digest that Ab/Original ancient peoples are the oldest living people on this planet and their culture was intellectually supreme to all others, it is no wonder that there is a deafening silence regarding your research. . . . Nothing much positive is accepted in Australia about Aboriginal people and you and your father's books are exceptional in content re: Aboriginal Australia. Thank you for bringing our ancient culture and the people to world attention."

—Associate Professor Rosemary Van Den Berg

"I enjoyed reading your book and was sorry to read the tale of persecution of the indigenous people of Australia. It is the same tragic story among indigenous people in North, South and Central America, Africa and India as well. Your information about the origin of humanity being from Australia is interesting. Geneticists will no doubt determine the truth of it over time. If the Dogon did come from Australia originally then they likely brought their beliefs from there. My research points to the Dogon religion as being as close to the first religion that we are likely to find on the Earth. This is because they were isolated and virtually untouched by the Europeans until the 1930s. Unfortunately once contamination takes place, the original mythology begins to change. If the elders in Australia were able to maintain their original beliefs, it would be nice to learn more about their teachings. Thanks. Shannon"

—Shannon Dorey, author and researcher

"This book makes an admirable attempt to establish that the original stock of modern humans evolved 'out of Australia' and not 'out of Africa' as Establishment science presently insists. Being an author and 40+ year researcher on evolution, human history and related subjects, I rated this book 5–star for the following reasons: 1) The story of human evolution presently taught in the schools of advanced nations is deeply flawed . . . the proof is abundant for any honest person with an open mind to consider. 2) This book does a fine job of adding fascinating evidence which adds to the open debate. While my personal investigation has led me to a somewhat different conclusion from those arrived at in this book, I fully concede the authors have made some startling analysis which is difficult to refute. Thanks to the courage and original thinking of the authors mankind is getting closer to understanding the true story of human history."

—Robert Steven Thomas, author and researcher

OUT OF
AUSTRALIA

OUT OF AUSTRALIA

Aborigines, the Dreamtime, and the Dawn of the Human Race

STEVEN and EVAN STRONG

HAMPTON ROADS

Hampton Roads Publishing Company, Inc.
Charlottesville, VA 22906
Distributed by Red Wheel/Weiser, LLC
www.redwheelweiser.com

Sign up for our newsletter and special offers by going to
www.redwheelweiser.com/newsletter/.

Cover design by Jim Warner
Cover photograph © Neftali/bigstock
Interior by Deborah Dutton
Typeset in Adobe Caslon Pro and ITC Franklin Gothic Std

ISBN: 978–1–57174–781–5

Library of Congress Cataloging-in-Publication Data available upon request

Printed in Canada

10 9 8 7 6 5 4 3 2 1

Warning to peoples of Australian Original and Torres Strait Island descent: this book contains the names of deceased original Australian elders (surnames withheld)*

It is our privilege to be able to share some ancient Original Australian truths and paradigms that run contrary to the accepted version of Original pre-history. The Original Australians were the great philosophers and spiritual mystics of much earlier times, and it was from these people and their culture that the nobler traits of modern human civilization arose. They were the first *Homo sapiens* and their genes played a vital role in the evolution of modern humans. And it is from the continent of Australia and its Original people that a new world history and legacy will be remembered and reinstated. Our role is to relay and validate their ancient account of times long ago, as told by representatives of the oldest continuous culture on this planet.

> "The aboriginal race of Australia is the only race which, in my opinion, could serve as the common ancestor for all modern races."[1] (Sir Arthur Keith: *Adam in Ochre: Inside Aboriginal Australia*, 1956)

---

* Australian Original = Australian Aboriginal

CONTENTS

ACKNOWLEDGMENTS

First and foremost we wish to thank Dellene, wife to Steven and Evan's mother, for her support, patience, and just being there.

Very Special Thanks to Elders: Auntie Bev and Karno for their guidance and help in Original matters and Lore.

Thanks to John McGrath for forcing us to investigate the Dogon.

A special thank you to those who helped us on and off site, all volunteers and at their own expense: Sean, Nina, Lavinia, Binnah, Adam, Jim, David, Paul and Phoebe, Fiona and Mark, Sarah and Richard, Erik, and Gavin.

Deepest respects and appreciation to Original Elders and Custodians: Auntie Minnie Mace, David, Jarmbi'je, Iris, Darren, Scott, Rob, Kevin, Gloria, and Mark.

Last and by no means least, we want to thank Jan Scherpenhuizen, our editor, publisher, and cover illustrator and designer. Words literally fail us in trying to express how integral Jan has been in editing, guiding, supporting, and for all intents and purposes, being so much a part of how we write and our future improvement. If we had our way his name would be alongside ours, as co-writer. Without Jan as part of our team none of this would have occurred. Our eternal thanks and deepest gratitude.

INTRODUCTION

We cannot claim that this book was conceived as a single project with a unified plan. Rather it grew organically, as a series of articles. Only after completing the last chapter, originally fashioned as a magazine article with a 3,500 word limit, did we begin to recognize a common thread and the potential for something more ambitious. This encouraged us to dip into our files of unused material and flesh the work out further, strengthening the theme we had begun to discern and adding to its internal coherency. Whatever changes were brought about in the development of this volume, they were informed by the touchstone that governs our every written word. Whether examining archaeology, historical accounts, or ancient religious teachings, the spirit of the Dreaming remains our yardstick.

Though often referred to as a religion, the Dreaming is much more than a collection of metaphysical concepts and moral prohibitions. It is the spiritual beacon which provides the societal and personal guiding light to every Original soul and tribe.

The Dreaming's genesis is a time before time began when the earth was soft. In this eternity dwell the Creation Spirits who gave form to this unformed reality. But the Original understanding of chronology is not that of naïve Western science, and the Dreaming is not a period of formation that is now over but one that is infinite. Indeed, one term for the Dreamtime, *Alcheringa*, has been translated as—to see things eternal. It is obvious that, in trying to come to grips with the ineffable, words can only get us so far. However, to some extent we can say that the Dreamtime is a place, a time, and a vision; one which is all places and all times; a dimension of reality which creates and sustains, and provides purpose and meaning.

Yet, in the Original paradigm, this highly mystical concept is thoroughly grounded, for the Creation Spirits manifest through the land which shares this eternal reality. Every person and place in the continent is embraced by these beings (or we might say, this Being). The Creation Spirits determined all personal and tribal identity, relationships of respect and the ways of communicating with them. They defined the relationship with non-human species and the land, initiation ceremonies, cosmological tales, and every other aspect of life (and death) imbued with deep meaning. These form an eternal circle whose source is the Dreaming.

The integrity of the Original spiritual paradigm is guaranteed in perpetuity because of its comprehensive nature; one which is untainted by the materialist and competitive influences of the degenerate societies which have replaced a similar vision. That vision was, doubtless, once worldwide and, as we shall see, was probably initially exported from Australia. Whatever true spirituality exists in the world only does so insofar as it retains some essence of this original teaching and taps into the vision behind it.

The integrity of Original spirituality has proven itself by being maintained over many millennia. There is no room for change when one sees things eternal. There is no motivation to modify a lifestyle and societal structure which has manifestly demonstrated its efficiency and stability.

It has often been asserted that truth is the first casualty of war. In their self-serving efforts to justify the multitude of crimes perpetrated against Australia's Indigenous people, the invaders have whitewashed their own actions and created a tissue of lies. In rationalizing the slaughter of the Original people, the theft of their land, and their attempts at cultural genocide, Europeans have characterized them as the most primitive and "miserablest people on earth."[1]

In some cases the invaders actually thought that the people they found in the new land were indeed inferior. Although there were those with eyes to see, too many were blinded by the lack of what they perceived as civilization—something resembling the products of Ancient Babylon or modern Paris—to recognize true civilization when they saw it. They forgot, or chose to ignore the fact, that there would have been no Babylon without war, thievery, and slavery, just as there would have been no European grandeur without the slaves of Greece and Rome, the feudal system, the plunder of crusades and pogroms, and the rape of the rest of the world in the "Great Period of Colonial Expansion." Spirituality, in such a world, whatever core of true guidance and vision it retained, was thoroughly compromised by the power elites who infiltrated (and in some cases established) its institutions. "The Great Religions" (or at least those "of the Book") have been distorted and transformed into tools of control and repression.

In contrast to this, the Dreaming has been able to maintain its integrity because Indigenous Australian society is not molded by these exploitative, violent, acquisitive aims and therefore has no motivation to distort the truth. Untainted by the separatist consciousness of "Modern Man" the Original Australians realize that to betray the Dreaming is to betray themselves. To rent the truth is to rent their own flesh. To destroy the land is to destroy themselves. To exploit or suppress another human being is to do violence to one's self and repress one's own finer nature.

When one really lives in the spirit, eternally, and sees it in the land and all things, then there is no chance of becoming disconnected from it and truth and morality—for at base all of these are one. This is why Australia, in the years before Cook, is the only continent where there were no wars of conquest, there was no slavery and no confiscation of chattels (not that the Original people are attached to acquiring and holding onto material goods). For all of these reasons we are convinced of the absolute and unchanging nature of ancient Australian truth and that it forms an important source of knowledge to be considered alongside that gleaned from Western science and history.

Accordingly, there are two complementary roads we choose to travel upon: the empirical and mystical. In the most general terms, each chapter of this book focuses on one theme, and is drawn from information found in our three previous books,[2] on our website *forgottenorigin.com*, and from our most recent research and discoveries.

Close to half of the content addresses the archaeological and historical evidence in support of our contention that the people of ancient Australia played a key role in the development of spirituality and culture throughout the ancient world. We, along with every custodian of Original Australian lore we have made contact with, are adamant in our shared belief that the Original people "don't come from African people, we are not related to them at all."[3]

In Chapter One we will be looking at how, despite the absolute accord amongst custodians of ancient lore and their resolute defense of a separate ancestry, the generally agreed upon conventions of science and academic history place the origins of *Homo sapiens sapiens* not in Australia, but Africa. The widely held belief that Africa was the first location from which modern human beings evolved then spread across the lands, as established by some of the most recent advances in science and mitochondrial comparisons, is assumed to be a done deal. However, there is no possible way any form of genetic study will give up a specific location. That is to say, all we can determine is where the oldest remains of a specific racial type is found, not where its ancestors ultimately came from. Yet, on the current evidence, according to many researchers and scholars, the oldest *Homo sapiens sapiens* remains are found in Australia.

We will see how two of the seminal researchers in the field, Alan Wilson and Rebecca Cann, were forced to back away from their original statement that Eve's place of birth was "probably in Africa"[4] solely due to compelling new evidence made available through advances in the scientific unraveling of DNA.

A second group of *Homo sapiens sapiens* did not emerge in Africa until about 40,000 years ago, long after their Australian predecessors were well established. There is a substantial amount of empirical evidence directly supporting the idea that there was a migration of ancient Australians in large boats voyaging from their homeland to a variety of locations throughout the Indian-Pacific Ocean Rim. All manner of proof was discovered with apparent ease, which was both a surprise and cause of some despair to the old guard; photos of Ainu Elders and Indian children of today; the morphology of ancient pre-Clovis skulls found throughout America, so similar to that of the Original Australians; the bounty of Egyptian relics littered throughout Australia, along with many more discoveries, all pointed to the need for a radical review of accepted ideas and the prevailing academic inertia.

In Chapter two we look more deeply into the evidence of ancient Australian mariner's having reached the far reaches of the globe. We consider the fascinating find of the "Hobbits"[5] of Flores Island and the documented existence of a race of little people native to Australia. We will see how the term "Original Australian" is misconceived, for it is used to cover a subject far more diverse than most would suspect. In ancient times there were no less than three distinct original types of *Homo sapiens sapiens* sharing the continent. Alongside the original type most Australians are familiar with, the "gracile type,"[6] and the little people, there was a "robust"[7] type with highly distinctive features of its own. The presence of three such distinct strains, given current theories of the length of time it takes for dramatic mutations to develop, in accord with established evolutionary theory, gives further weight to the antiquity of the Original race. An examination of the extensive evidence drawn from the analysis of the blood of Original people only adds confirmation to the case. Finally we will be looking at how the explosion of Mount Toba 74,000 years ago would have left ancient Australians with a large advantage over any other races present in the world at that time, creating an opportunity for their expansion and exploration of the world.

In Chapter Three we consider the wealth of information coming out of the Americas testifying to an extremely long history of contact which stands in open contradiction to any Out-of-Africa theories. Dates of 40,000 years have been attached to unmistakable evidence of modern human activity occurring at Topper (South Carolina) and Lake Valsequillo (Mexico). These were the subject of heated debate and derision no less than a decade ago. In what only compounded this fairly recent inconvenience, it has now been stated, by well-credentialed experts, that all skulls of the more ancient type of American display a "look most similar to . . . more like that of Australian Aborigines."[8]

We will be making the case that there is so much evidence in support of our theories that the laws of probability themselves would seem to mitigate against our thesis proving incorrect. We examine the academic and political machinations that seem to play a much bigger role in obstructing the acceptance of the Out-of-Australia Theory (OAusT) than genuine scientific objections.

Chapter Four focuses on the evidence for an ancient *Homo sapiens sapiens* presence found within Australia itself and some of the little known technical accomplishments of these people, including seafaring and astronomy. We consider the vital testimony of the Elders of the Original people and what light the Dreaming stories have to shed upon the history of the land.

In Chapter Five we will commence our look at the massive spiritual influence the original perspective has bequeathed to the world. Given the endemic ignorance and prejudice with which Australia's original inhabitants are viewed by many Westerners, we can anticipate that it will be asked: so what if ancient Australians had ventured beyond the shores of the Great Southern Land? What could the impact possibly be of this ancient migration of naked hunter/gatherers who bore stones, bones, and sticks and an aversion towards farming, mining, and banking? However, as we will have shown and will demonstrate further in later chapters, Original culture was nowhere near as lacking in technological sophistication as those who have sought to destroy it have either assumed or pretended. But beyond the knowledge and skills relevant to the mundane world that Original Australians possessed, what they had to offer of a spiritual nature is, if anything, even more significant.

We are of the opinion that until about 8,000 years ago, the Dreaming was the global inspiration behind all religions and the first attempts by modern humans to grapple with the complexities of life and death. Flourishing for millennia before the advent of glyph and letter, this ancient oral mythology, along with many ceremonies and traditions, was rapidly forgotten as the forging of the plow and changes in lifestyle marked a parting of the ways. Unlike the rise of cities and farming in the new world, which was dutifully recorded, the culture of the original peoples was obliterated or ignored, leaving only traces of their inspiration to be detected or surmised solely by those willing to exercise perception free of prejudice. There is no religious tradition anywhere that acknowledges any such influence, yet the authors of this book aim to show that, despite the obvious additions to and redefining of the original paradigm by subsequent authors, there is more than ample remaining that bears the unmistakable insignia of the Dreaming and can still be found within all religions, past and present.

We will outline nine basic principles which can be detected within the paradigm informed by the Dreaming and examine how these can be found in Egypt and the Middle East, implying the influence of Original Australian thinking and perception. Dreaming concepts and values can be detected in Pantheism and Gnosticism, the concept of the sacred feminine and the figure of Mary Magdalene. A comparison of Genesis and Dreamtime creation myths is also instructive in this regard.

Chapter Six continues our examination of the Original spiritual legacy. We dive deeper into the well of evidence of contact with Egypt, considering the practice of mummification within Australia, similarities between Egyptian and Original words and hieroglyphics and pyramids found in the bush. A comparison of the mystical traditions of the Isiac and Dogon religions with their source, the Dreaming, is instructive. It makes evident that reference to the oral mythology and ancient lore of Africa confirms what is already strongly indicated by our examination of the evidence drawn from studies of mtDNA, Y chromosomes, and the physiognomy of skulls found in other locations.

We will maintain that, however many similarities between ancient metaphysical systems and the dreaming may be found, the purity of the application of the message is determined by one overriding aspect: the management of the resources of the land.

The spirits of the Dreaming are in and of the land. Ancient Australia and the lifestyle which reigned there are quite literally the source from which all legends relating to the Garden of Eden originated. Yet it is with the fall that the two traditions part company.

Clothed and ashamed, Adam and Eve were banished from paradise, and proceeded to till the land. The previous state of harmony was lost to be replaced by one in which mankind were pitted against nature, prey to wild beasts, and forced to eek out a living by the sweat of their brows. Meanwhile, naked and proud, they remained within the Edenic tribal estate upon which they are destined to reincarnate life after life.

The extensive reforming of the landscape, the building of roads and dams and cities, all of what developed civilizations see as the hallmarks of their advancement and superiority, are, in terms of the Dreaming, the signposts of the fall.

Chapter Eight expands upon those principles among the nine principles of the Dreaming mentioned in chapter five that remain unexamined so far. We consider the Original concept of reincarnation and their metaphysics of time. For them, time is circular with no beginning or end. Life repeats in an endless return and one lifetime is merely a staging point and opportunity to prepare for the next incarnation. Death is no more than the last ceremony before discarding the flesh. The eternal cycle is all that ties the individual to the universe. Original Elder, David Gulpilill, summing up this endless connection with the Spirits and the Dreaming, expressed it like this:

> To the Aboriginal, death is not the end of life. Death is the last ceremony in this present life. Then the soul is reborn, thus all living people are reincarnations of the dead. The soul lives on and finds a new body to inhabit. This belief in reincarnation provides a direct link back to the ancestors of the Dreamtime.[9]

We look at the prominence of serpent worship around the globe and how it relates to the Australian Original people's Rainbow Serpent, "the longest continuing religious belief documented in the world,"[10] according to Josephine Flood. We consider commonalities in shamanic practices of initiation and trauma and the relationship Walkabout has to meditation as a vehicle for solitude and contemplation.

Chapter Nine records the magnificent yet tragic tale of the Original people of Tasmania. Perhaps more than any other, this shows how incapable Westerners have been of understanding and appreciating the value and nature of a mindset foreign to their own. The Tasmanians were misunderstood as the most primitive of all people due to their austere lifestyle and lack of material goods. However, their asceticism demonstrated their spiritual richness rather than their material poverty. To consider them poor would be the same as to consider sahdus—the naked holy men of India—as primitives because they chose a similar lifestyle. It is to be blind to what an achievement it is to live in a harsh environment without clothes and on a limited food supply and thrive as these people did, in tune with nature, themselves and the cosmos.

We will see how their technology was misinterpreted and how the fierce resistance they offered the invaders shows they were far from a dispirited, disorganized primitive rabble. If an ability to deceive and betray is the mark of civilization then, indeed, in this the white man showed his superiority as we chronicle the eventual demise of this proud and wonderful nation.

Sadly leaving the nation of sahdus behind, in Chapter Ten we round out our examination of original spirituality with a further exploration of Original shamanic practices and the Original people's attitude to death.

In Chapter Eleven we pick up the story of the Original people's technical and cultural achievements which are so little known. Among the many things ancient Australians had knowledge of were brain surgery, amputation, penicillin, the construction of axes and bows and arrows, sailing, navigation by the stars, burial, and communication with dolphins. Chapter Twelve looks at Original cultural accomplishment in art, language, and the calculating sciences.

Chapter Thirteen considers the whitewash of the white invasion. The greatest tragedy in relation to restoring the truth of Ancient

Australian history is that there is no end to the distortion and paternalism which began when the British hoisted the Union Jack on the soil of the Great Southern Land. The lies have continued since, unabated. They had to as the act of proclaiming the land a British colony was founded upon a flagrant abuse of the International Law of the times, and in direct defiance to the orders Cook was expected to obey. The only way the myth of *terra nullius* could be justified was through an institutionalized vilification of the land's inhabitants and a pernicious cultural genocide, to say nothing of the horrors inflicted upon the inhabitants of Tasmania.

In spite of the piecemeal nature of this book's compilation, there is a common thread that was revealed with hindsight and is consistent with what Elders and custodians of ancient lore have said since the Dreaming and Creation first began. These chapters are all essentially part of the same story; the scenes may vary but the theme remains the same: the Original Australians were the first modern human beings.

Undeniably, some of what follows sits well outside what is assumed to be fact, and there have been occasions where some of what was discovered or revealed has caused us to raise our eyebrows. Curbing our reflex urge to omit or rephrase, we remain ever-alert to preserve an eternal truth, the source of which we rely upon being of the highest order: the authentic oral accounts and ancient Dreaming stories that come directly out of the mouths of the people who witnessed these events. Passed on, generation after generation, the sacred nature of these teachings plus the absence of any incentive to tamper with tradition, seems to us to be as close to a guarantee of pure truth as one is likely to get. It was such an honor to hear of these tribal treasures that the mere thought of desecrating the narrative and, therefore, the wisdom of the Elders and their Spirits was impossible to conceive. There is no higher source.

To those stuck in the Western scientific materialist mindset, in which spiritual ideas are mere fancy at best and cynical concoctions designed to manipulate and control at worst, this is impossible to understand. But for those to whom the Dreaming is a felt reality, it is just as hard to understand how it can remain unperceived. The materialist sees a dancer but cannot hear the music to which she dances and therefore thinks her a fool. To the dancer the materialist is simply, in some bewildering way, tone deaf.

The Dreaming is the binding principle that enshrines the rejection of conquest and insists upon equality between all the "products of nature."[11] Thus, it forges a link between the ethereal and the earthly. It was the principles of the Dreaming that ensured that the history of an entire continent was unmarred by episodes where one group stole another's country or resources, until the white invader introduced a new set of values. The Original people most assuredly squabbled over petty issues and behaved poorly at times. That is the human condition, irrespective of geography, but in spite of the imperfections inherent in *Homo sapiens sapiens*, all lived the same lifestyle, used the same technology, went naked without shame, eschewed personal wealth, and never took possession of or moved onto another tribe's land.

We are convinced that, while we must appreciate all we have today, comparing it to what was originally offered by the First Australians is of vital importance in deciding upon which path to travel tomorrow. Some may argue that all of this is ancient history, but any such judgment is solely dependent on perspective and ignores the sacred understanding of the world. If time, and life itself, runs along a straight line with a finite start and finish, then our contribution to the understanding of the world is, at best, destined to occupy a small strand in the curriculum of some senior history courses. However, if time is circular, as Indigenous Elders maintain, and merely different expressions of cycles in repetition, then the custodians of ancient lore may well be correct in insisting their ancient ways will come again.

This book represents an attempt to broaden the range of colors on the palette of history. While scholars and students alike seem to have an insatiable appetite for regurgitating the "wonders of the classical world" and the exploits of European kings and conquerors, a shameful vacuum persists when it comes to acknowledging the ancient legacy of the Original Australians.

It is a conventional maxim that one must study history to avoid repeating its mistakes. And yet the study of those who instituted the colosseum, the inquisition, holocausts and gulags doesn't seem to have led to the building of a world without war, pillage, and greed. In fact, the same policies of relentless expansionism and motives of acquisitiveness have seen the sovereignty of other nations continually ignored under the guise of a war against terror and nations raped by banks (who will as happily prey on their own people as other nationals). So endemic is this culture of greed and crime that while these outrages are generally acknowledged, there is no expectation that the guilty will be punished as they own the government, the military, and the courts. To say nothing of the environmental threats that could see an end to life on this planet if a different course is not taken.

Psychology has, until recently, mainly concentrated on the ill, reasoning that, by understanding the sick mind we will find ways to cure it. However, there is a growing interest in studying those who exhibit exceptional mental health in order to discover their secrets and how others can benefit from adopting the attitudes and practices that lead to peace of mind. By the same token, what better way to work toward a harmonious lifestyle than by studying those people who, in their natural state, have been recognized as the happiest in the world? A people who lived in harmony within themselves and among one another, without war, slavery, and exploitation and in harmony with the environment and all the creatures of the land.

We have made it our mission in the course of the following chapters to raise general awareness of the variety of skills and depth of knowledge present in this continent well before the British invasion. Most importantly we desire to impress upon our audience the richness of Original spirituality that the world has had as a precious resource since the dawn of the awakening of real consciousness. A richness which is available to them still. We wish to awaken in our readers an understanding of the true history of this land, and indeed, the world, and share, as directed by custodians of lore throughout the country, what really happened, what should have been, and most importantly, what still could be.

CHAPTER 1

THE "FIRST RACE"[1]

Over the last decade, all manner of unexpected archaeological discoveries have led to many experts questioning much of what was assumed to be fact. A large variety of unexpected findings have called into question many elemental assumptions held about the past. These include the discovery of little "hobbits" on Flores Island; Siberian hominids with mtDNA connections to the people of Papua New Guinea (PNG); and the purity of our distinct genetic *Homo sapiens* code being compromised by a Neanderthal component of 4%.

Professor Clive Gamble of Southampton University succinctly summarized the current impasse and polarization this has caused, when declaring we have to construct "a completely new map of the world and how we peopled it."[2] Granted, our response to Gamble's call may seem radical; however, these discoveries, found not only in America but throughout the entire Indo-Pacific Region, all point to the same ancient southern location as the key to the new cartography.

After extensive consultation and research, we are of the opinion that at some time in the distant past, no less than 50,000 years ago and possibly much earlier, Original men and women set sail from Australia and began exploring foreign lands. They were the bearers of new insights and options, and bequeathed humanity their genes and the cornerstones of a genuinely civilized civilization: religion, culture, gender equality, art, sailing, democracy, astronomy, and surgery.

Australian Original guardians of traditional Lore and Law have made it clear to us that they are indeed the "First Race."[3] Over the millennia the First Australians watched as other nations and lifestyles emerged and squabbled, but they always kept themselves apart, rejecting all societies focused upon the individual or the material. They were not, as assumed by some of the general public, ignorant savages stagnating in a state of primitive inertia. As highly respected *Dhungutti* Elder, Rueben Kelly, stated, their role was to maintain an esoteric presence in a world increasingly blinded by bright lights and all manner of material temptations. "Centuries ago you white people chose the path of science and technology. That path will destroy the planet. Our role is to protect the planet. We are hoping you will discover that before it's too late."[4]

Unlike others out in the field or laboratory, the authors of this book have "discovered" nothing: our role is to act as scribes and faithfully present the history of the Original Elders. The rest is easy: find white-fella proof to substantiate black-fella truth.

Before we can begin to paint the canvas depicting ancient Australia's true heritage, it would be best for us to try to tear down the screen of the Out-of-Africa theory (OAT) which has kept it hidden from sight for so many years. According to academics and archaeological texts, Africa is the place where modern humans evolved before spreading their genes throughout the continents. OAT has, over the years since it was first proposed, been transformed from a hypothesis into a fact. One of the original papers that lay claim to charting our ancient ancestor's movements and origin "The Recent African Genesis of Humans" was written by Professors Alan Wilson and Rebecca Cann and was widely acknowledged as the closing chapter in this mystery. However, as we noted in our introduction, amongst the absolutes proclaimed was one qualifier that has been conveniently and repeatedly overlooked. The authors stated *Homo sapiens sapiens* "probably"[5] evolved in Africa, and now, with the benefit of hindsight, we can see that the qualification was a wise one.

Wilson and Cann proposed all modern humans shared the same ancient mother, who they named Eve. According to their calculations she lived in Africa sometime between 150,000 and 200,000 years ago. Of crucial importance are two of the three assumptions that underpin their mathematics. "The aboriginal [sic] populations of New Guinea and Australia are estimated to have been founded less than 50,000 to 60,000 years ago. The amount of evolution that has since occurred in each of those places seems about one third of that shown by the whole human species. Accordingly, we can infer that Eve lived three times 50,000 to 60,000 years ago, or roughly 150,000 to 180,000 years ago."[6] This declaration was regarded as the final word, and the resolution of "15 years of disagreement"[7] between two branches of science. Wilson and Cann triumphantly proclaimed victory on behalf of the molecular geneticists declaring that "we won the argument, when the palaeontologists admitted we had been right and they had been wrong."[8]

With the case closed and bragging rights secured in perpetuity, science had once again provided certainty in regard to an African ancestry. Or so it seemed, but not long after their paper was published, Rebecca Cann realized they were mistaken.

Cann and Wilson's analysis focuses on the mitochondrial DNA (mtDNA) present in bone and blood samples. These genes are passed on from mother to daughter and are the most reliable evidence to draw on when determining the age of a particular race. MtDNA is far more reliable than the nearest male equivalent, the Y chromosome, and more predictable in its progression. Each new strand resulting from mutation appears at a set rate and the more variations apparent in a sample of DNA the older the race.

However, Cann and Wilson's paper was based on observing evolutionary markers they assumed were apparent which were not actually based on examination of the DNA itself. In 1982 Cann actually examined the mitochondrial DNA of 112 Indigenous people, including twelve full-descent Originals, and the results were in total opposition to what they assumed was fully resolved. Cann was obliged to contradict the basic conclusion of their first paper, by stating that "mitochondrial DNA puts the origin of *Homo sapiens* much further back and indicates that the Australian Aboriginals arose 400,000 years ago from two distinct lineages, far earlier than any other racial type."[9] Cann not only asserted that the emergence of Original *Homo sapiens* was "far earlier"[10] than any Africans, she suggested a new point of origin of the species and a revised chronology of racial evolution. "The Australian racial group has a much higher number of mutations than any other racial group, which suggests that the

Australians split off from a common ancestor about 400,000 years ago. By the same theory, the Mongoloid race originated about 100,000 years ago, and the Negroid and Caucasian groups about 40,000 years ago."[11]

The realignment and reversals were of immediate concern to Alan Wilson. If Cann was correct in detecting a "much higher number of mutations"[12] they might as well tear up their original paper. Determined to resolve the obvious inconsistencies, Wilson made two visits to Australia. In 1987, Wilson sampled the mtDNA of twenty-one full-descent Australian Originals and identified fifteen different strands. This equates to a 70% mutation rate, well above that of any race.

A second visit in 1989 gave up even more data that forced Wilson to abandon his belief that Africa was where *Homo sapiens* originated. A second sampling of the DNA of ten full blood Originals found a similar percentage (70%) of mutation present. Upon receiving the results of his second mtDNA sampling, Wilson immediately conceded that the OAT was wrong.

The math wasn't complicated: the agreed rate of mtDNA mutation for every new strand is 3,500 years; therefore $22 \times 3,500 = 77,000$ years. Wilson realized if he returned to Australia and increased the population surveyed, the likelihood was that he would find more mutations and the date was likely to be pushed back even further.

"It seems too far out to admit, but while *Homo erectus* was muddling along in the rest of the world, a few erectus had got to Australia and did something dramatically different—not even with stone tools—but it is there that *Homo sapiens* have emerged and evolved . . . *Homo sapiens* would have evolved free from competition out of a small band of *Homo erectus* 400,000 years ago."[13]

Sadly, and somewhat puzzlingly, these findings were mostly ignored. In fact, opposition to OAT lost momentum. Perhaps this conservative climate goes some way towards explaining the reactions to Alan Thorne's research into the genetics and antiquity of Lake Mungo Man (WLH3). Re-dated to be over 60,000 years old and the oldest *Homo sapiens* yet found, this discovery in itself raises serious doubts about the validity of any theory claiming the first mariners reached the northern parts of Australia 60,000 years ago. This date, coupled with the discovery that WLH3 had an "extinct DNA"[14] which does not resemble that of any other population, surely calls into question the reality of an African migration.

Referring back to Wilson and Cann's original calculations, their proposed timing of between 50,000 and 60,000 years ago for the settlement of Australia stands on no less shaky ground than their genetic miscalculation. There are at least nine Australian sites claimed to be older than 60,000 years (see the table below for a quick summary). Granted every date is challenged by conservative critics, but even so, all those proposed are the result of work by respected academics. What needs to be accepted is that if just one date proves to be correct, irrespective of whatever judgment is passed on the other nine, it can be confidently declared as a fact that Australia was not settled by African *Homo sapiens* 60,000 years ago.

LOCATION	ACTIVITY	YEARS
Lake George	Fire-stick farming	120,000
Lake Eyre	Skullcap	135,000
Jinmium	Tools	176,000
Panaramitee	Rock-engraving of saltwater crocodile	75,000
Rottnest Island	Tools	70,000
Devonport	Rock-engraving	>115,000
Jinmium	Art	75–116,000
Great Barrier Reef	Fire-stick farming	185,000
Lake Mungo	WHL 3 complete skeleton	61–65,0000
Lake Mungo	WHL 1 cremated bones	61,000

THE FIRST AMERICANS

The recent discoveries of "hundreds of skeletal remains"[15] in America that "look like Australian Aborigines"[16] indicate that early immigrations were more likely from Australia than to it. In the October/November 2011 edition of *Cosmos*, Jacqui Hayes presented a compelling morphological case in support of there being an Australian Original presence in America. According to Hayes, Original settlement of the Americas began at an indeterminate time before the second migration of people "with distinctive Mongoloid features,"[17] and that "startling new finds suggest Australia's first people made it all the way to South America more than 11,000 years ago,"[18] This leaves an unresolved question. How far back did these Original settlements span, and were other locations settled? If, indeed, Hayes is right, in that Australian Original people were the first to enter America, any artifact or indication of human activity dated as more than 11,000 years old must be related to people bearing Australian Original genes.

The impossibility of any ancient African migration to America having occurred was confirmed through the examination of Original bones that established the presence of distinctive antigens. "Arnaiz-Vilena and his team looked at the human leukocyte antigen (HLA) system, which is a group of proteins on the surface of human immune cells. The HLAs are what doctors test for to determine whether one person's tissues are compatible for organ or bone transplants. HLA is a nuclear marker giving an even genealogy and genetic history for both sexes. The best test showing that HLA is a good genetic marker for studying population relatedness in that it usually correlates with geography."[19]

As expected, the first nominee was Australian, but just as importantly the comparative results bore witness to one genetic type which was notably missing; it seems the Africans forgot to sign on for this distinctive genetic marker. "So what did they find? Unique signatures only found in Australian Aborigines, Pacific Islanders, and peoples in Asia and even in Europe."[20] The non-appearance of African HLA is yet another inconvenient piece of evidence for anyone wishing to hold onto the theory that Eve was an African.

When factoring in these recent additions to the Australian Original/American time line, dates just exceeding the maximum Clovis (Mongoloid) entry date are certainly inconvenient to established theory, but do not demand tearing out pages from standard text books . . . yet. There is a substantial amount of corroborating evidence of Original presence in the Americas during the 10,000 years before the second migration from Asia began. It can be found at Tlapacoya, 21,700–25,000 years before present (BP), Los Toldos Cave, Patagonia, 14–15,000 BP, "Meadowbank Rockshelter 19,000 BP (southwest Pennsylvania), Tibito 14,400 BP (Colombia), Walker 15,000 BP (Minnesota), and Mud Lake 13,450 BP (Wisconsin)."[21]

But it doesn't stop there. Professor Silvia Gonzalez, who is a leading advocate of the Out-of-Australia Theory (OAusT), was "quite staggered"[22] by the dates obtained when analyzing the footprints found in a layer of volcanic ash at Lake Valsequillo (Mexico). "A variety of prints (human and animal) captured in this layer of rock were dated using optically stimulated luminescence (O.S.L.)."[23] She found, much to her understandable surprise, that 40,000 years was established as the "last time that these sediments were lit by the sun's rays or the last time that the material was heated."[24] Gonzalez is adamant these are Australian Original footprints, and that they were left by people who reached America by boat by "island hopping"[25] around the Pacific Basin.

Such a date, 40,000 years, pushes the boundaries and affirms the reality of an extensive Original tenure in the Americas. Nor is this an isolated bit of evidence. The corroborative timing of Albert Goodyear's site cannot be a coincidence, and its significance is strengthened by the considerable distance between locations. "Goodyear had been working at an archaeological site on the Savannah river, near Topper. It was agreed all the available evidence from the Clovis site had been gathered and their work was complete . . . He kept digging for another four metres before an assortment of stone tools, along with a hearth, were unearthed. A small piece of charcoal was then analyzed by counting the residual Carbon 14 and a date of no less than 37,000 years was deemed appropriate."[26]

Uncomfortable as these dates are for anyone clinging to traditional theories in relation to when ancient Australian Originals first came to America, for such individuals it gets worse. Not far from the Lake Valsequillo footprints Gonzalez investigated is another site that was deliberately ignored for close to thirty years after a comprehensive investigation was conducted by Cynthia Irwin-Williams. The dates are so sensational and numerous, and so obviously associated with objects made by *Homo sapiens,* the archaeologists downed their tools and clipboards and vowed never to return. The dates returned by a variety of sound geological analyses were far too ancient, not only for a presence in the Americas, but well outside the assumed period when *Homo sapiens* first appeared on earth! To some extent the issue isn't just a matter of whether these numbers are feasible, it is more a case of open antagonism between two competing branches of science.

Christopher Hardaker, author of *The First American*, created a fictional conversation between the two competing parties which graphically highlights how much the argument over which group of academics have the right to exclusively claim victory has blinded the combatants.

> ARCHAEOLOGIST: You are asking us to believe that the sophisticated art and technology of the Upper Paleolithic was actually invented over 200,000 years ago in Central Mexico by *Homo erectus*? Ridiculous.

> GEOLOGIST: You are asking us to believe that Science is off by a magnitude of 10? Ridiculous.[27]

Often the result of cutting-edge technology, the chemical analysis and computations came from extremely reputable institutions and individuals. Some of the techniques performed upon the layer of volcanic ash and debris deposited above the artifacts and footprints which delivered the offending dates include Uranium Series Dating

(200,000 years); Zircon Fission Track (170–640,000 years); mineral solutions (200,000 years); Diatom analysis (80,000 years); U-Th/He (200,000 years); tephrahydration (250,000 years); magnetic shifts in rocks (790,000 years); and argon argon (1,300,000 years). The facts, and large figures, demand a response. What if just one date is actually right? Does that mean *Homo sapiens* were, as Christopher Hardaker claims, responsible for "600,000 year old art?"[28]

As to whether Gonzalez' "island hopping"[29] route from Australia, up through Asia, Japan, Siberia, then America is plausible, it is often said a picture can act as a worthy substitute for quite a few words. A photograph of a Japanese full-descent Ainu Elder was taken in the late nineteenth century by German anthropologist, Dr. Hermann Klaatsch. The physical characteristics displayed in this photograph are strikingly similar to those of an Australian Aborigine. As are those of "a very well-preserved skeleton from Gua Gunung, Malaysia,"[30] which was recently discovered and about which it was reported "[this] specimen is aged 10,200 B.P. and is said to be a late representative of a non-specialized morphology, similar to Australian Aborigines."[31]

THE FIRST BOAT

For traces of a population "similar to Australian Aboriginals"[32] to be present in Malaysia, Japan, America, or any other place, a boat is needed. The oft-proposed settlement of Australia from Africa by ramshackle raft, or through desperately clinging on to driftwood during storms, doesn't measure up. This vessel must be able to withstand monsoons and weeks at sea. It must accommodate a crew of close to twenty adults so that the settlers in their new home can avoid in-breeding and successfully populate an uninhabited continent. Nowhere today is anyone going to discover the actual ancient wooden remains of such an ancient sophisticated "ocean-going"[33] vessel. However, if there is no actual wreckage to be found, there is, nonetheless, other evidence of a seafaring tradition among the ancient Australians.

Graham Walsh was "the widely recognized authority on the intriguing Bradshaw art of the Kimberley area . . . Within this area, he has discovered the oldest paintings of boats in the world, dated at a minimum age of 17,000 years, but with the strong possibility of being up to 50,000 years old . . . Walsh insisted that the"[34] "high prow of the boat"[35] is "unnecessary for boats used in calm, inland waters. The design suggests it was used on the open ocean."[36] Walsh was quite shocked by the function, antiquity, and most importantly, dimensions of these vessels: "they are massive boats, totally alien."[37] Moreover, not only was the sophistication and technology exhibited difficult for Walsh to assimilate, he still had to account for the reasons why there were "two paintings of ocean-going boats, one with 23 people on board, the other 29."[38]

These are ideal numbers for founding populations sailing towards distant lands. However, diagrams and specifications of themselves do not make a boat. To have a clever idea is a promising first step, but there are some practicalities to be addressed before an actual nautical expedition can be embarked upon. There are materials, tools, and navigation skills required which supposedly did not exist for at least another 20,000 years. Irrespective of what is assumed, the first tool needed to build a ship that can comfortably cater for thirty people is an axe. Wood in its prime, not the rotting logs that fall by themselves, is essential in manufacturing a vessel strong enough to sail across oceans.

It should come as no surprise that the oldest axe in the world, dated as 40,000 years old, was found at Huon Terrace P.N.G. (which was part of the Australian mainland until 8,000 years ago). Others discovered are also incredibly old, like the examples found in Jaowyn land, Northern Territory (35,500 years), at Sandy Creek, Queensland (32,000 years), and Malangangerr Northern Territory (23,000). All of these are at least 8,000 years older than the first axe found outside Australia, at Niah Cave, Sarawak, which is dated as 15,000 years old.

With axe at hand, plans on the wall, and overseas bookings made, there still remains one vital seafaring skill any journey beyond landfall demands: navigation. Hugh Cairns's book, *Dark Sparklers*, is the first and only publication dedicated to the sharing of traditional Original astronomical knowledge. Cairns won the trust of *Wardaman* Elder, Bill Harnley, who spoke of his ancestral knowledge of the stars, "great black shapes"[39] the movements and constellations in between, and of up "on top."[40] According to Cairns, there have been Original astronomers for "over 30,000 years."[41]

Not only the Pacific, but the Indian Ocean, was navigated by ancient Australians who brought many esoteric gifts, technologies, guidelines and, of course, their genes to distant continents. "Dr. Raghavendra Rao and researchers from the Indian-backed Anthropological Survey of India project found unique mutations were shared between modern-day Indians and Aborigines."[42] They "identified seven people from central Dravidian and Austro-Asiatic tribes who shared genetic traits only found in Aborigines."[43]

Much earlier linguistic studies of the Dravidian language had already identified a relationship between the two peoples. Dravidian "fishermen of the Madras coast use almost the same words for I, thou, he, we, and you as some Aboriginal tribes. Many other key words in the Dravidian dialects are identical to Tasmanian Aboriginal terms both in pronunciation and meaning."[44]

"It needs to be appreciated that Tasmanian culture and language is a relatively recent event, and the island is the outcome of the final thawing at the end of the last Ice Age when the seas covered the low plains between Victoria and Tasmania. Over the last 8,000 years this isolation has been instrumental in the development of a distinctive Tasmanian culture."[45] With a language that came into existence no earlier than 8,000 years ago forming a substantial part of the basic Dravidian vocabulary, this mtDNA connection strongly suggests the Australian Originals kept in contact with India for some considerable time. The cultural connection is further emphasized by the fact that "Australian canoes are constructed identically to those of the coastal Dravidian tribes of India, and wild tribes in the Deccan region of India are the only culture known to use the boomerang outside Australia."[46] The oldest boomerang discovered in the world was found at Wyrie Swamp, South Australia, and is dated at 10,200 years. That the dingo is accepted to have been brought into Australia from somewhere in Asia about 6,000 years ago only strengthens the possibility of a history of extended Australo-Indian interaction being fact. It would appear that the Dravidians adopted the Australian boomerang to hunt with, chose their better designed canoes to assist in fishing and, as is often the case when two cultures first meet, shared technology, friendship, and genes.

There is so much more to this history of the dissemination of ancient Original culture. At best we have provided a brief geographical overview of where ancient Original people sailed, and hopefully presented evidence validating their belief that they are descendents of the "First Race."[47] Whether or not the African strand of *Homo sapiens* emerged 40,000 years ago is of no account; our focus is on the much earlier Australian genesis, journeys, and heritage. We have examined a few of the locations reached, but as for the religious legacy of the Dreaming as evidenced through the nine shared spiritual principles, underpinned by equality of gender and species, that is yet another chapter of an ancient story that spans eons and the geography of the planet. Their intimate awareness of the divine was bestowed upon the world, along with lesser gifts: seafaring, astronomy, brain surgery, penicillin, burial/cremation/embalming, amputation, the making of the axe and bows and arrows, democracy, and so much more. This is all part of a hidden legacy of forgotten origin that deserves to be uncovered once more. We will be turning our attention to these matters in later chapters.

CHAPTER 2

AN EXTENDED FAMILY

In our first chapter we made reference to mtDNA research that stands in direct opposition to the Out-of-Africa theory. Professors Alan Wilson and Rebecca Cann suggested then rejected an African genesis of *Homo sapiens*. Both conducted further independent mitochondrial studies which led them to reposition humanity's point of origin out of Africa and into Australia.

The apathy and disdain that followed was due to a mixture of archaeologists steadfastly defending established dogma and a chronic inability to think outside the box. According to prevailing expectations, Wilson and Cann failed on two elemental counts. First and foremost, the case was already closed; the scholars were satisfied that Africa's credentials were secure. For Wilson and Cann to be right, irrespective of what genetic anomalies they identified, we have the supposedly ludicrous notion of *Homo erectus* sailing across 100 kilometers of ocean in a vessel carrying no less than twenty adults around 400,000 years ago.

It is widely accepted that *Homo erectus* was capable of making tools and possibly made fire, but when it comes to the higher achievements such as art and creating ocean-going boats, these have always been considered as exclusively the province of *Homo sapiens*. The theory of origins revised by Cann and Wilson, if correct, contradicts nearly everything written in texts and taught in schools in relation to human pre-history.

However, there is plenty of evidence that some major rewriting of the history books is overdue. In 1999 (eight years after Wilson died), Michael Morwood conclusively proved that not 400,000 years ago, but nearly 1,000,000 years ago, *Homo erectus* was indeed constructing large boats capable of sailing considerable distances. Not only did his discoveries at Flores Island introduce a new species of hominid of an antiquity never anticipated by experts but, furthermore, the island of Flores is the second closest to Australia. Such convincing evidence of *Homo erectus's* nautical prowess led Josephine Flood to concede that not only were "*Homo erectus* voyages closer to Australia,"[1] but this fact "also makes evidence for an earlier human arrival of ancient mariners into Australia easier to accept."[2]

Morwood found evidence on Flores Island that intelligent hominids (either *Homo sapiens* or erectus) sailed there sometime between "800,000 and 900,000 years"[3] ago. "The dating is reliable—volcanic tuff deposits from above and below indisputable stone artefacts and associated extinct fauna were securely dated with the well-tried and trusted fission-track method."[4] The island was separated from Indonesia by 20 kilometers of ocean and "three deepwater straits,"[5] and had never been joined to the mainland. Irrespective of whether these mariners were of the species sapiens or erectus, to successfully populate this island requires an initial influx of no less than twenty adults (to negate in-breeding). If, at a later date, the numbers became too large for the resources of the island to sustain and some continued onwards in their southward journey, these explorers would next step ashore at Timor. Beyond Timor, if still heading south, all that remains is one large southern continent: Australia.

The entire scenario is plausible, especially so when we factor in the minor improvements required if sailing longer distances in a boat of the same seaworthiness and dimensions as that which reached Flores. The modifications needed to sail an extra 80 kilometers when given over 400,000 years to lift the prow and strengthen the structure are not beyond the abilities of these explorers. Equally, it is possible these hominids sailed from Australia, first reaching Timor, then Flores. Regardless of the original point of departure, a boat was in action hundreds of thousands of years before any such vessel was thought to have been invented.

THE LITTLE ORIGINALS

Of course Morwood's work on Flores not only raised new questions about *Homo erectus's* capabilities and its role in the development of the human world, it also introduced another member of the hominid family into the discussion: the little people. Referred to by the press as "hobbits," these beings, despite having a cranium capacity smaller than chimpanzees, had a culture, constructed tools, and spoke and behaved no differently than those of a taller stature. What are we to make of this? Were they an aberrant strand of erectus, a genetic abnormality, or the result of living in a tropical climate? These are but some of the explanations offered. Where they came from, their relationship to other hominids, and how they got to this island at least 100,000 years ago are issues beyond the conventional understanding of the universities, but they present no problems to the Original custodians of ancient lore.

It is already known that a race of small Original people existed in Australia, as evidenced in a 1938 photograph of a Barrinean male adult standing alongside archaeologist Joseph Birdsell. Highly regarded by neighboring tribes, they were renowned for their wisdom in esoteric matters. They "developed sophisticated techniques to remove poison from tropical plants"[6] and constructed "sturdy domed huts—the most elaborate structures in the whole continent—that gave protection from rain and lasted for several years."[7] They played with "a unique, cross-shaped boomerang, which was used for sport and games rather than hunting."[8] These small Original people lived in the rainforest in the hills behind Cairns, Queensland (QLD). Two months after the photo was taken, the Barrinean tribe of over 100 people, who were disheartened by the current state of affairs, walked off into the rainforest vowing never again to make contact with white society. Since that exodus they have not been seen by non-Originals, but their presence and genes never quite disappeared. The local primary school is renowned for the extremely high proportion of children well below the expected height range for their age. Elders have also been in contact with these little people but are very guarded in regard to sharing any details.

Some, if not all, non-Original commentators made the mistake of assuming the Barrineans are the sole representatives of their kind in Australia. Many have proposed the tropical habitat had a part to play in gradually lessening the height of this unique race of small Original people. It is an uninformed opinion indicative of a lack of faith in the comments made by Original Elders, and equally, poor research. Over 1,000 kilometers to the south of Cairns, a tribe of forty-three little Original people were still living in the foothills behind the Gold Coast in 1864. An account of the massacre of the Dhi'lami is as distressing as it is prophetic and justifies the Barrinean tribe's decision to sever ties with the invaders.

A firsthand account of the aftermath of this atrocity begins with the chronicler being woken by "much gunfire"[9] which led to him witnessing the "most despicable act of humanity."[10] The author was left utterly devastated.

> Bastards! Bastards! . . . What manner of animal could do such atrocities to another human being?" He "recognized these were the Dhi'lami little people of . . . previous acquaintances . . . killed part decapitated and hanging over a tree branch—the son less his manly wares . . . none had survived. This last group of the Dhi'lami were all quite dead, 43 members of the clan, as I had counted . . . their scrotums cut away . . . found six young boys and six young girls of the near ages of 9 to 12 . . . brutalized in most cruel manner similar to their mothers . . . blood streaming from their front and rear orifices. Bastards! Bastards! . . . emptied my churning stomach of its full contents.[11]

An extremely intriguing account compiled seven years earlier declares that "this was the land of the left-handed little people called the Dhin'dharri-dha' pen,"[12] and also makes mention of their numbers exceeding 100. Their stature was markedly different to that of the neighboring tribes; being "rather smaller than all other natives"[13] the Dhi'lami were "more stockiere yet remaining wirely thin . . . stomachs bulged prominently . . . pronounced body hair . . . long chest-length beards . . . deep-sunk eyes with large foreheads."[14] And in what resonates to the same sentiments often expressed when describing the countenance of the Barrineans, they were admired by Originals and sympathetic whites as bearing a "mystical personage."[15]

The similarities between the Dhi'lami and their distant northern cousins do not end at their size and mystique. Surely it cannot be coincidental both tribes of little people used the same distinctive multi-layered means of communication. The Dhi'lami's "strange speech came forward in very soft tones . . . almost a whisper . . . they commenced to converse with each other not using language . . . communication was in hand gestures and tongue "clicking."[16] When hunting, "not a sound was made . . . their movements were silent— rarely a leaf rustle was heard."[17]

The *Bundjalung* Language Confederation of 13 Tribes have many Dreaming stories detailing their interaction with little people, which they call bittars. Many an Elder has made special mention of the bittar, insisting they still exist. But the story doesn't end there. It involves all of Australia and lands beyond. When leaving these shores, we suspect Original people of varying height and stature were seated in many boats. These small Original people were settled throughout the continent, as was another strand of *Homo sapiens* commonly referred to as robust Originals.

THE ROBUST ORIGINALS

These were men and women with exceptionally thick bones, receding foreheads, and thick continuous eyebrow ridges. They displayed features markedly different from the gracile, fine-boned Originals present when Cook sailed up the east coast. The last of their species was found at Cossack, Western Australia (WA) and the 6,500-year-old date is claimed to mark off the end of the robust people's tenure, which spanned no less than 40,000 years. The biggest problem their existence creates for any Out-of-Africa theory relates to WLH50.

Having the most robust and ancient skull yet recovered, the morphology, dimensions, and shape of this large-boned individual are extremely different to those of other hominid species. If the conventional OAT was valid, they would share the same African ancestry. However, the mere 10,000 years that separates the remains of the two branches is insufficient time for two such distinct species to emerge, given the theory of gradual and random mutation that is the basis of accepted evolutionary theory.

As Josephine Flood remarked when comparing the features of WLH50 to other robust remains, the skull "is massive: he is so robust, he makes Kow Swamp man look gracile! The cranium is extremely wide and approximately 210 millimetres long. The cranium vault bone averages 16 millimetres thick."[18] With a "flat and receding"[19] forehead and the "archaic"[20] characteristics at the back of the "wide"[21] skull, some may mistakenly assume this individual represents a primitive strand of *Homo sapiens*. Nothing could be further from the truth. WLH50's brain is massive, far greater than any other *Homo sapiens*, "well above the average 1300 for modern skulls."[22] With a 1540-millimeter brain capacity, a powerful physique and huge bones, any comparison to WLH3, which has a skull thickness of 2 millimeters, is tantamount to likening an "orange peel and eggshell."[23] Not only does the gracile WLH3 bear an "extinct gene"[24] that cannot be linked to any African, its nearest homeland compatriot in age is the most robust Original yet found. As noted above, the anatomical differences at this stage, not long after disembarking on the northern shores of Australia, if sourced from one quite recent genetic base, should be barely noticeable. Variations of this magnitude, when the proposed immigrants are all of one race and began settlement in the same general area, should be the outcome of a great expanse of time or a huge difference in environmental factors. That the oldest and most robust individual found in Australia has the largest brain and thickest bones is an insurmountable stretch in logic if claimed to be from the same stock as the gracile Originals.

Nor is all of the evidence derived from the feminine mtDNA evidence. The male side of the equation, revealed through the study of ancient Y chromosomes, needs to be factored in before assessing any theory attempting to explain the genesis of modern humans. When we do so, it become increasingly difficult to comprehend how the obvious can be so cavalierly dismissed, as the notion of one homogenous African group sailing to Australia, irrespective of whatever timing is suggested, is not in accordance with science. The expectation was that this isolated population of African pioneers would develop "variations in Y-chromosome DNA in parallel with mtDNA variations."[25] This is a pattern repeated in every other population analyzed outside Australia, but within Australia there are "two haplotypes[26] unique to Australian Aboriginals."[27] Without laboring the point, it is worth noting that the word "unique"[28] is frequently invoked when comparing Original remains. The analysis of the genes of peoples outside Australia "produced 41"[29] haplotypes, whereas "most (78%) Aboriginal haplotypes fell into two clusters, possibly indicating two original, separate lineages of Aboriginal Australians."[30] Not for the first time has the notion of two distinct lineages been raised, but perhaps even the acknowledgment that the gracile and robust are indeed separate strands (if assuming habitation of Australia occurred 60,000 years ago) is still in need of one further point of elaboration.

These findings don't factor in the third part of this Original trilogy. The little people must also be related to both the gracile and robust populations. If the original ancestors arrived 400,000 years ago, such an evolution into three distinct strands is feasible. If they stepped ashore 60,000 years ago, the emergence of three dramatically different races that span the outer limits of *Homo sapiens* physiology, skull shape, and height is a very difficult proposition to sustain. Therefore, to maintain the integrity of the OAT, despite the obvious anomalies, common sense must be sacrificed on the altar of mediocrity, and all three strands have to be sourced from one small group of African mariners who sailed to Australia around 60,000 years ago.

ESOTERIC SCIENCE

One would expect the most recent developments in science, particularly in the field of mitochondrial research, have finally resolved the issue of humanity's genesis, and so it has. The comparative mtDNA studies of Wilson and Cann are not isolated findings, and as inconvenient as the research and results supplied by eminent Australian scientists and academics may be, all points and conclusions lead to the same ancient place of origin and genetic line of descent.

One of the very first intensive studies of Original mtDNA was conducted by Roy Simmons of the Commonwealth Serum Laboratory. His brief was simple: to determine where Original people originated from. Simmons had the good fortune to be able to analyze Original blood collected between 1923 and 1971 by Joseph Birdsell and Norman Tindale. Within this blood bank was the blood of 900 full-descent Originals and 1,500 with a small percentage of non-Original parentage. During the time this blood was originally sampled and tested, the sophisticated research techniques available to Simmons were unknown. Simmons's analysis was extremely thorough, and "for good measure, he paid particular attention to the question of any possible Australian connections to Africa. Repudiating the 'Out of Africa' theory of human origins, Simmons said that he thought that the Australian data indicated that the Aborigines actually evolved earlier than the African Negroes. There was no blood evidence, he said, to indicate the African Negroes or Negritos had any connection to the Australian Aborigines."[31]

Keith Windschuttle, a highly respected conservative historian who could never claim to be an advocate of Original culture or people, was as adamant in denying any African influence, but considered the geographical extent of the exclusion even more extensive. "Fifty years of blood genetic research . . . has failed to provide any clue to Aboriginal origins . . . May I state here and now that our extensive blood grouping surveys conducted in Australia, Indonesia, Melanesia, Micronesia and Polynesia over three decades have produced no genetic evidence that the Negro ever entered the Pacific."[32]

The genetic studies that maintain the difference of Australian Originals from Africans are so numerous, consistent, and convincing, Josephine Flood was compelled to admit that the "DNA studies . . . all support a common origin for New Guinea highlanders and

Australians. Aboriginals form an extremely ancient lineage, most different from Black Africans."[33]

What may surprise many is that not only the mtDNA found in Original blood, but conclusions drawn from a study of blood groups further emphasize the lack of connection between the two races. In the simplest terms there are three ways of categorizing blood, and "uniquely, full-descent Aborigines lacked A2 and B of the ABO blood group system, S of the MNSs system and Rh negative genes r, r' and r". Western Desert people show a distinctive genetic pattern, with the world's highest value in the N gene of the MNSs system, implying a very long period of isolation."[34] In complete opposition to the idea of any outside genetic influence is the analysis of blood that shows the above characteristics highlighted by a "long period of isolation."[35] This gives no comfort to anyone claiming an African connection to Australia. As Josephine Flood conceded: "Aborigines belong almost exclusively to A and O . . . Tellingly, in blood groups Aborigines resemble Caucasians."[36] Professor Lanarch, when presenting the findings on his extensive comparisons of the morphology of ancient skulls throughout the world to those of Australian Originals, was just as adamant in denying any African ancestry. The measurements were unequivocal and led Lanarch to conclude "we therefore have no hesitation in omitting Negritos as ancestors of the Australian Aborigines."[37]

THE VOLCANIC VACANCY

Enough of the blood and bones. There is evidence from an ancient eruption, which makes any claim of a rapid exit from Africa and entry into Australia impossible to explain if one is to rely at all on common sense. The catastrophic eruption at Mount Toba (Indonesia) was the largest of the last 2,000,000 years: "when the Toba volcano in Sumatra erupted 74,000 years ago . . . This enormous eruption spewed ash to the north-west, covering India, Pakistan and the Gulf region in a blanket 1–3m deep . . . and spread as far as Greenland . . .

this catastrophe reduced the world population to between two to ten thousand."[38]

As for Australia, situated in the opposite direction to the north-west, it is quite conceivable that it was the only continent to escape the fallout. Therein lay the opportunity for Australian Originals to explore lands now left open for settlement. The academics claim most of the few survivors were located in the very south of Africa and in the northern extremes of Europe. Previously, calculations in relation to numbers and localities assume Australia was uninhabited, and as such, when discussing the collateral damage, the population of Australia is immediately discounted from being relevant to any hypothetical census.

Apparently, according to every expert, the Gulf Region and the entire Asian subcontinent was almost completely depopulated. Why would the few remaining Africans be in a hurry to go anywhere? Nearly everyone was dead, most of the land and resources were uncontested, and the need to relentlessly spread their seed and acquire territories wasn't present. It has to be remembered, all human societies, according to the experts, lived a hunter-gatherer lifestyle until 10,000 years ago. Their needs were simple: realistically the only reason to move on is because of some depletion of resources or hostilities with neighbors. With neither pressure existing, why would these same people push on from Africa to the southern extremes of the Asian subcontinent to launch off into the yonder, without sign of land or any apparent reason to undertake such a hazardous journey?

A stretch of logic, undeniably, but it gets worse. Ignoring the genetic evidence and various conflicting facts, one would assume that once these African seafaring people, whom Josephine Flood called "beach-huggers,"[39] stepped ashore some 60,000 years ago, they would stick to what they knew and gradually settle along the northern coast of Australia. Once established and familiar with the unknown flora and fauna, they might then have slowly moved inland. There are nine sites that predate this hypothetical entry date (eight are over 1,000 kilometers south from any proposed northern point of arrival). All of them, despite being supported by substantial evidence, have their validity challenged by critics. Bearing in mind, if just one site is valid, the OAT is not.

What took place at Lake George over 120,000 years ago, if Gurdup Singh was correct, is ample proof no African entered this continent. Singh extracted core samples from the bed of Lake George, New South Wales (NSW) dating back 4,000,000 years. The pattern of deposits remained constant for 3,880,000 years and then literally went haywire. Some relatively minor species of trees, primarily eucalypts, almost overnight became an iconic part of the Australian landscape. From 120,000 years onwards there was massive increase in charcoal accumulation. The fact that the peaks in charcoal were associated with higher lake levels only narrowed down the list of possible agents who might be responsible. During greener times with a wetter climate, the incidence of fire multiplied. Conversely, drier vegetation and droughts saw the charcoal accumulation lessen considerably, thus ruling out the possibility that the increase in charcoal was due to natural causes. Singh had no doubt it was due to human intervention and evidence of firestick farming.

So ends another small chapter of an endless story that has an unexpected twist: this time the esoteric and scientific sit comfortably on the same page.

CHAPTER 3

ANCIENT ORIGINAL AUSTRALIANS IN AMERICA (A CLOSER LOOK)

With the question of whether or not the first mariners were Australian Original answered in the affirmative and a departure point established, it seems it is now appropriate to examine one port-of-call in greater detail. There is one continent, and one specific site which has seen careers ruined, and contradicts the fundamental understandings underpinning today's accepted version of *Homo sapiens'* prehistory and genesis. The headline of the October/November 2010 edition of *Cosmos* magazine and its accompanying byline, featuring a photograph of an American skull (Luczia) exhibiting morphology that resembles Original people, highlights the current controversy surrounding the recent discovery of many skulls that bear Australian Original bone structure.

"Did Aborigines discover America? Startling new finds suggest Australia's first people made it all the way to South America more than 11,000 years ago."[1]

Undeniably the banner and article written by Jacqui Hayes addressed issues rarely spoken of in Australian academic circles, but the tone of the article was somewhat timid. When concluding her analysis of a wide cross-section of "two different groups of people,"[2] of which "the oldest human remains look like Australian Aborigines,"[3] she offered two possible explanations. The uncertain climate in which these theories were suggested was epitomized by the fact that her suggestions were put as questions. "Could it really have been the common ancestor of Australian Aborigines, or even the Aborigines themselves? Could they really have taken the onerous voyage across the Pacific in flimsy craft, or braved the Southern Ocean to reach the tip of South America?"[4]

Prominent archaeologist, anthropologist, and biologist Associate Professor Walter Neves is of the opinion these people were part of a larger group that first emerged from Africa and split, with half veering south to Australia while others continued on until settling in America. In support of this less revolutionary scenario, Neves has made it clear that irrespective of whatever date is agreed upon, the Australian Original people were unable to sail these distances. They were bereft of the sophisticated skills needed to construct and navigate "ocean-going"[5] boats. But the Ramindjeri are adamant this is untrue. Nor are they alone. Corroborating evidence can be found in many Dreaming stories; and as we saw in previous chapters, further corroboration comes from the study of Dravidian genes, photographs of Ainu Elders, ancient Malaysian bones, paintings of "ocean-going"[6] boats spread throughout the Kimberleys, and the bones of Original Australians discovered throughout America. Marsupial bones unearthed at Siwa Oasis, Egypt, add yet another piece of fascinating evidence to the picture which we will be returning to later. In choosing between the views of one esteemed academic and those of a group of traditional custodians, as we have had to on previous occasions, the same choice is both compulsory and unfailing.

It now seems that America was merely one outpost of an Ancient Australian immigration, and that the second wave of immigrants who are recognized as the indigenous people of America appeared on the horizon much later, around 10,000 years ago. That they were the second group to enter this continent does not lessen their claims to land and lore, as we are convinced both the Australian and Asian settlers abided by the principles of the Dreaming and lived harmoniously until a decreasing gene pool started to impact upon Australian numbers. Nevertheless, the Original Australians did arrive much earlier, and it is reasonable to assume every site which shows indications of *Homo sapiens* activity that returns a date exceeding 11,000 years reveals the presence of Original Australians. Evidence of Original Australian occupation doesn't have to take the form of actual bones. Anything, be it tools, art, or footprints, is sufficient proof of presence.

The term *Homo sapiens*, when used in this ancient American context, must be reworded, as the description is too general and should include the point of origin and genetic heritage of the subject: Original Australian *Homo sapiens*.

There are compelling ancient archaeological discoveries from a particular Mexican site that return dates and carry implications, that have ruffled the sensibilities of many scholars, and have literally destroyed friendships and careers. Unofficially, proclaimed as a "black hole"[7] for close to thirty-five years, the archaeological evidence in dispute, found at Lake Valsequillo, is agreed to be of *Homo sapiens* making. Past that solitary point there is no consensus, and often bitter debate.

The dates coming out of Lake Valsequillo break all the rules and contravene conventional timelines charting the ascension of *Homo sapiens*, and in what seems a bizarre twist, the dispute is not due to a challenge from some upstart from an obscure branch of fringe science overstepping their subjunior jurisdiction. The ongoing polarization of opinions between academic camps is primarily a disagreement between advocates of the most recent advances in dating geological formations and eminent scholars versed in many fields of archaeology. Quite simply, dating of the geology in which the artifacts and other evidence was found at Lake Valsequillo keeps returning six figures, while the defenders of traditional archaeology have only just begun to accept the possibility of five figures being possible.

What staggers us is that irrespective of which of a variety of techniques were applied, whether utilizing uranium, argon-argon, zircon, or tephrahydration, the resulting dates are uniform in running into hundreds of thousands of years. Nonetheless, the conclusions have been challenged, and have been a source of irritation ever since Juan Armenta Camacho first noticed "a bone sticking out of the hardened sediments"[8] near the shore of Lake Valsequillo in 1959. Originally Camacho mistook this enigmatic artifact to be yet "another mineralized fragment from an old elephant,"[9] and paid no special attention until cleaning the specimen that night. "Then he saw them:

engravings of exotic animals, such as a feline figure with seven spears running through its body, a serpent's head, a tapir, a short-faced bear, and several types of elephants."[10]

As unexpected as these carvings were, what caught everyone's attention was the carving of an "incredibly ancient gomphothere, a four-tusked cousin of the mastodon, recently given a cameo appearance in *Lord of the Rings*. It was gone from the States a million years ago,"[11] and thus, sat outside the parameters of every migration theory accounting for America's first people. In what only compounded the inconvenience, "the art had been engraved when the elephant bone was still fresh, still 'green.' The elephant and the other animals pictured had all died out at least 10,000 years ago."[12] Of course, this way of framing the problem gives the most conservative estimate of when the carvings could have been made—10,000 years ago. It doesn't take into account the antiquity of the gomphothere and that the carvings could have been made at any time during which the beasts existed hundreds of thousands of years ago.

Despite the carving bearing what are obviously ancient subjects, the reactions were mixed. Many academics were decidedly hostile, but there were others who were prepared to pick up their clipboards and trowels and step into the void. Acclaimed as "a perfect team for a perfect archaeology,"[13] the experts assembled were investigating a site lacking in ambiguity or problems. Cynthia Irwin-Williams "was chosen as lead archaeologist for the 1962–1966 Valsequillo project"[14] and in total there were fourteen of the most respected academics selected to make sense of this anomaly. Everything on-site was so promising: the artifacts and bones were found in-situ in a "mappable geological formation of streams and volcanic deposits,"[15] there was a distinct gradation in tool sophistication, and in what separated this site from any trace of Clovis technology "the spearheads were more primitive than the earliest accepted projectile points made by the 12,000 (year) Clovis hunters."[16]

And so the dig began, and once completed, it was more than thirty-five years before anyone dared to venture into an area that rapidly became an unofficial forbidden site for any academic who wished to publish, teach, or simply remain employed. The art and technology recovered are universally agreed to be produced through the activities of *Homo sapiens*; everything else is open for debate or avoidance. The problems began once the individual tests of the various materials laid over the artifacts at a later date were published, the numbers just didn't add up, and the proliferation of noughts was beyond anyone's expectations.

Barney Szabo was the first to upset traditional archaeological sensibilities. His speciality is analysis through Uranium Series Dating, and he was convinced "the artifact beds were in excess of 200,000 years old"[17] and held to this belief while under some considerable peer pressure over many decades.

Shortly after, a second corroborating paper published by another member of the Valsequillo team, Virginia Steen-McIntyre, did momentarily stoke up the beginning of a serious academic debate. Chosen primarily for her expertise in tephrahydration, for which her paper received a Ph.D. at Harvard, Steen-McIntyre became a tireless and principal advocate for the extremely ancient dates her analysis produced. Tephrahydration is a recent and highly regarded advance in dating through calculating the amount of "water absorbed by volcanic glass shards, in tephras"[18] (layers of volcanic ash and pumice). When the volcanic matter cools, the glass shards form bubbles of gas which are trapped inside. Over time, water is absorbed and seeps into the minute spaces. The underlying premise is quite logical: the more water present in the glass shards, the older their age. "Comparisons of the percentage of water in the bubble cavities to the percentage in the tephras of known age suggests an age of about 250,000 years for the Valsequillo tephras."[19]

Not long after, a third paper detailing the application of zircon fissure-track analysis on the tephra units above the artifacts, conducted by Charles Naeser (USGS Branch of Isotope Geology) presented a range of dates between 170,000 to 600,000 years. This paper, and the earlier two, seemed to tip the scales and led to an extremely brief period of earnest debate and spirited discussions. Naeser is highly qualified and respected, as are his two colleagues. His research was cutting-edge and has proven to be very accurate. His analysis of two different materials, Hueyatlaco ash as being 370,000±200,000 years old and Terela brown mud as 600,000±340,000 years old, even when factoring in the inherent wariness most scientists possess when making absolute declarations, carried with it a high degree of certainty. Naeser stated that "there is a 96% chance that the true age of these tephras lie within the range defined by the age and plus or minus value."[20]

These results were but some of many, but paradoxically, together they added up to very little when it came to changing established beliefs. From the time the first result was announced, there was one overwhelming obstacle in the form of two archaeologists who did their best to see that the whole issue was summarily dismissed and that researchers would move on to more important business. To begin with, the principal archaeologist, Cynthia Irwin-Williams, absolutely refused to publish or endorse any of the startling findings. She did nothing other than disclaim the discoveries and accompanying dates when her colleagues ignored her promptings, which provided quite a hurdle to their acceptance. She advised all of the researchers against publishing any paper proposing such radically unconventional dates as "every reputable pre-historian in the country will be rolling in the aisles."[21] But in the background was an even more dominant player and a formidable foe of the new findings.

Marie Wormington was the undisputed matriarch of American archaeology and one of the most strident critics of the ancient dates. It is well known that Wormington had chosen Cynthia Irwin-Williams as her protégé and was actively ensuring she would eventually take her mantle and uphold the status quo. Wormington made it clear the dates were ridiculous, end of story. Wormington's aversion towards even raising this topic was extreme, and her concern for those sullying her chosen successor's name was even greater. She confronted the principal nonconformist, Virginia Steen-McIntyre, at a San Francisco archaeology conference and accused her of "ruining Cynthia's career!"[22] Her response really did highlight both the extent of the academic divide and which camp was indeed using clinical research as its standard. Her defense of "a reckless and damning accusation [she] had to contend with for decades"[23] was simple, "I was just doing science."[24]

Very soon after everything went quiet, with the exception of Virginia Steen-McIntyre's dogged insistence the dates at Valsequillo were valid, little was heard. For her part the rebel was accused of the unforgivable faux pas of going public "with crazy dates."[25] She was speaking with the press and general public, pleading the case for her science (and that of many others), but within the mainstream of academia, Steen-McIntyre was barely tolerated and mostly ignored. In another odd twist in this strange case of academic myopia, the engraved bone found by Camacho mysteriously disappeared. In 1990 Irwin-Williams began to do something she vowed she would never attempt. Personal papers, thousands of slides, and all manner of reports were gathered together in preparation for writing her long-awaited paper on Lake Valsequillo. Then she died. Soon after, all her papers, photographs, slides, and evidence were collected by the appropriate people then promptly lost or misplaced. And so things vanished or stagnated, until the appearance of a maverick who came out of left field in 2001, with a self-funded six-week dig at Lake Valsequillo.

Marshall Pyne is an MIT graduate with degrees in engineering and business whose views are untainted by the ongoing squabbles that arise between geologists and archaeologists whenever the finds at Lake Valsequillo are raised. He made sure to contact the most respected and liberal-minded academics willing to analyze material taken from the same site left vacant since the mid-60s.

The second time around the results were no less controversial. Employing not only strategies previously used but also bringing into play refinements to existing techniques and forms of analysis unknown in the early '60s, the results only confirmed what Szabo, Naeser, Steen-McIntyre, and others had already determined. Of all the new research "perhaps the most exciting is the data presented by Sam VanLandingham on diatoms (microscopic fossils) from the artefact beds and overlying (younger) beds."[26] He found fossils of microscopic species that became extinct at least 80,000 years ago.

Yet despite the evidence continuing to pile up, there was no sign of the old impasse ending. The situation was best summarized by one of the dissenting underlings who defied Irwin-William's edict that the established dogma remain unchallenged. Charles Naeser succinctly presented the illogicality of their opponents' critique twice-over. "The question here is the relationship between the artifacts and the geology. All of the geologic evidence supports an old age for the artifact horizon. U-series, fission-track and U-Th/He dating as well as Sam's diatoms and Ginger's superhydration and mineral solution studies point to an age >200,000y."[27] The hurdle critics of these dates face if dismissing the underpinning science or methodology relates to the chances all geologists were mistaken. This possibility is remote and stands at odds of 6/1 (if just going on the small sampling provided by Naeser). The objections of Irwin-Williams, Wormington, and many others defy the laws of probability. As Naeser noted: "someone could probably find something in question about each of the geologic indicators of a 200,000y age. The problem is that it would have to be something different for each technique. No single argument can reject all of the geologic data. That rapidly becomes a geologic impossibility."[28]

The battery of tests used at Lake Valsequillo provided a variety of dates that began at 80,000 years, included many six-figured dates and the potential of "600,000–year-old art."[29] All that is needed to complete the picture and silence the critics is the discovery of a skull. If it wasn't for a stray bomb striking a section of the Leipzig Museum during World War II, that skull, and the case for a far more ancient American pre-history, would be accepted without question.

A *Homo sapiens* skull was recovered from the same site towards the end of the nineteenth century; it was acknowledged to be unique and of such importance the Mexican government used this discovery to cement political relations with the German/Austrian Ambassador. They presented the remains to him as a gift. Once arriving in Germany, it became the center of extensive research and public interest. It was named the Dorenberg skull and was proudly displayed in the Leipzig Museum until it was finally blown up. Fortunately, amongst the many investigations and records, one remaining slide of "extinct diatoms lining the inner surface of the skull"[30] was eventually found at the California Academy of Science by Sam VanLandingham in 1970. "He noted the presence of several species [of diatoms] that became extinct before the end of the Sangamon interglacial, 80,000 years ago, and so inferred the skull must therefore be older than that date."[31]

In a recent follow-up study, VanLandingham was sent samples of material collected by Steen-McIntyre from beds that contained bifacial tools. As has become the norm, his comparative study confirmed that the same minimum date of 80,000 years applied, and "found the same suite of diatoms in these samples as was found by Reichelt with the Dorenberg skull."[32]

Where does all this lead to? Before passing judgment, what needs to be factored into this debate is the lack of science or analysis the defenders of traditional archaeology bring to the argument. More than willing to attack the methodology and findings of many geologists, there has not been one opposing piece of research presented as an alternative, just quotes and reminiscing about long-dead mentors and theories originally penned by quill feather. In Australia, when Jim Bowler challenged Alan Thorne's revised dates exceeding 60,000 years for Lake Mungo Man and Woman, he chose to cite earlier research that was more to his liking. In America, time after time, the denials have exclusively followed the same line of argument—it just doesn't fit. All of the American geologists involved are highly credentialed and came to Lake Valsequillo with no cause to champion. Their brief was simple, to do "science."[33]

One of the central sites and planks upon which we based our dating of the finds and our belief in the origins of those responsible for them is, ironically, inspired by Professor Gonzalez's mathematics in relation to human footprints recently discovered in the volcanic ash at a different site at Lake Valsequillo. They are in the same general location, and once again archaeology is in dispute with geology. But there is one minor variation on this theme. Gonzalez's date, which she found "quite staggering,"[34] is indeed well beyond the limitations of mainstream expectations, but on this occasion the offending date was the product of one of their own.

Human occupation, of which Gonzalez is convinced was from Original Australian stock, beginning in America earlier than 40,000 years ago, is a bitter enough pill to swallow, especially so when the two dissenting papers on the same site are no less than twenty times more unpalatable.

Geologist Paul Rennie was engaged in a lively discussion with Silvia Gonzalez (*The Science Show*, ABC Radio, February 11, 2006) and was of the opinion Gonzalez's "staggering"[35] date underestimated the real date by a factor of between twenty and thirty times. Focusing on the magnetic peculiarities of the volcanic material analyzed, Rennie was somewhat bemused by Gonzalez's conservative calculations pointing out that "the fact that we found reverse polarity magnetisation in this rock tells us really without much further analysis that it is older than 790,000 years."[36] If that wasn't an issue in itself, Rennie also conducted a second analysis of which he was even more confident, noting that "the argon argon method is really the most reliable, accurate and most precise dating method that is currently available to date rocks in the tens of thousands to billions of years age range."[37] The resulting age estimate of "1.3 million plus or minus 0.3 million years"[38] is of critical importance in that not only is it the "most precise"[39] but this is the first time a date of seven figures had been so confidently attributed to evidence of human existence.

To her credit, Gonzalez was quite willing to concede that these older dates were the product of valid science, admitting that "the problem is we are dating different fractions of materials that are present in the ash. And what we need to do now is defer the dating to try and understand why we have these completely different answers; 1.3 million and 40,000."[40] Of course both of Rennie's dates are dramatically larger than Gonzalez's meager mid-level five-figured offering, but very much in keeping with what fellow geologists discovered at another site in the same basin. Of crucial importance when deciding whether geology or archaeology is closer to the mark is an observation made by Charles Naeser. With ten separate tests discussed (of which there are many others) examining all manner of residual reactions/deposits, all of which would have to be invalidated, we are left with no option but to adopt Naeser's stance in declaring the chances that Australian Original *Homo sapiens* were not at Lake Valsequillo at least 200,000 years ago is a "geologic impossibility."[41]

So who, when, and where does that leave us? If the geologists are right, the OAT isn't. Bear in mind, most of these dates relate to the layer above the artifacts, adding another nought; thus moving up into seven figures is not only conceivable but necessary according to the results of argon-argon testing. If just one of these ten dates is proven correct, does that mean there was more than one place from which modern humans evolved?

And if, as it now seems, these people were of Original Australian ancestry, sailing across oceans hundreds of thousands of years ago, what part of the accepted version of humanity's pre-history is not in need of revision?

CHAPTER 4

THE TOSS OF A COIN

The greatest problem we have faced when sifting through the inherent contradictions existing within the "science" of archaeology relates to the subjective nature of any academic discipline that claims certainty within a setting that reaches back tens of thousands of years. Over the last fifty years, according to the most creditable authorities, Original occupation was judged to have first begun in Australia 12,000 years ago, then 20,000, revised upwards to 25,000 years, and was soon followed by popular T-shirts proclaiming 40,000 years of settlement. From that agreed point, the timing of Africans first arriving in Australia has edged backwards in increments of 10,000 years, and just when all thought 60,000 years was the absolute upper limit, there is talk of the Africans reaching the northern shores of Australia 65,000 years ago. Such an erratic track record engenders little confidence in either the efficacy of the science or certainty in the pundits' next recalibration.

However, there is now an emerging body of evidence where there is less dispute, and on some occasions, something close to an accord in regard to a date.

Whenever discussing ancient Australian history and ancestry, before consulting those with a display cabinet full of degrees, we consider it mandatory to first determine what the keepers of traditional original lore declare as truth. We have been vigilant in always deferring to the wisdom of those who were here when such things actually took place. And in this respect whether the advice of Elders or hidden wisdom contained in an ancient *Bundjalung* Language Confederation Dreaming story, the notion of African involvement or any genetic ancestry abroad is addressed and dismissed.

Willay Bitjar (*Dhungutti* Elder) is adamant the Original Australian people are of the "First Race."[1] Moreover, having been in personal contact with Elders from the Apache, Inuit, Hopi, and other American indigenous tribes, Willay made special note of their shared admission that the Australian Original people were the "first to stand upon the Earth."[2] According to another Original spokesman steeped in ancient wisdom, everything began in Australia. "They say we have been here for 60,000 years, but it is much longer. We have been here since the time before time began. We have come directly out of the Dreamtime of the great Creation Ancestors. We have lived and kept the earth as it was on the First Day. All other peoples of the world come from us."[3]

Not only do "all other peoples . . . come from us,"[4] special mention is made of one locality in the *Gumbangirr* tribe Dreaming story, *The Frog who was King*. Surprisingly, the myth is extremely specific in nominating one forbidden continent: "Africa . . . That's where the lions and tigers are."[5] It is made clear everything African, whether the people or animals, was expressly denied entry into Australia, forever. So ancient was the setting of the story, happening "when the world was made, years and years ago,"[6] it details a series of rebuttals made when "another old fella came from the other side of the world. Where did he come from, Africa?"[7] Time after time the African king refused to accept no, and "the old fella goes back to wherever he came from,"[8] returning with another uniquely African offering/animal. No matter what was presented as an incentive, the "old king"[9] who "used to look after Australia"[10] responded with the same lie. "*Yoo, ngunee kunee walkung.*"[11] That means, "Yes, we got all those things there."[12] Finally discovering the deceit, the African king used his magic and turned the Original king into a frog. His sorcery did nothing to stop the embargo; every day this same frog, and his ever-increasing offspring, joined in the same chorus, "Ngunee kunee walkung. Gityeeng Boseeya." That means, "We've got 'em here in this place . . . O, we don't want anything like that."[13] Even though the myth takes the Australian king to task, "because he told a lie,"[14] owing to the fact the greater good was served, and all things African were permanently kept at bay, this deed will always be lauded simply because it "saved Australia from those deadly animals."[15]

So Original tradition is clear on this point: no Africans into Australia; the Original people evolved solely within the continent of Australia, and before anyone else. Moreover, if "all other peoples of the world come from us,"[16] they had to be the first *Homo sapiens* and must have spread their genes once sailing from Australia.

Having established what the Elders of the original Australians have to say on the matter, it is now appropriate to examine eleven sites in Australia which also render data that contradicts the notion that Africans did enter Australia 60,000 years ago.

NINE SITES (PLUS ONE)

The first site, and closest in age to the date of the assumed African migration into Australia, is found at Lake Mungo. The lake has been dry for over 15,000 years and is located to the south of the center of Australia, and well over 1,000 kilometers from any suggested African entry-site. Until quite recently the remains of a man and woman often referred to as Mungo Man (WLH3) and Mungo Woman (WLH1), were assumed to be around 30,000 years old. However, an extensive reanalysis of the bones of WLH3 through the use of three dating techniques, under the supervision of Drs. Alan Thorne, Rainer Grun, and Nigel Spooner, returned dates in excess of the cut-off point of 60,000 years. A date of 62,000 years was obtained both through Electron Spin Resonance (ESR) and Uranium Series, and in what must reduce considerably the odds of random chance or the potential of all three approaches being faulty, analysis by Optically Stimulated Luminescence (OSL) returned a date of 61,000 years.

Undeniably, the findings of this paper have met with criticism. Jim Bowler disputes the methodology behind the comparative study measured through OSL, and equally, although conceding the dating of Mungo 1 and 3 (WLH1 and WLH3) was in need of revision, is more comfortable with a shared date of 45,000 years. Although this version can accommodate an African settlement, it also refashions Bowler's strident denial into an each-way bet—more of that later.

Nominating a time barely 10,000 years earlier and focusing on a location thousands of kilometers to the south of any northern entry point, Charles Dortch's work at Rottnest Island (WA) has attracted virtually no interest, nor has an opposing paper been written to discredit his date of 70,000 years. For all intents and purposes his work has been ignored; however, the tools he discovered, undeniably of human construction, were found in association with charcoal at a time when every conventional theory claimed Australia was uninhabited.

Extending just a little further back in time, but again remaining within the bottom southern section of Australia and some considerable distance from the Top End of Australia, is an intricate rock carving of a crocodile's head which was "discovered" in 1923 at Panaramitee, Southern Australia (S.A.). Not only is it a fine piece of art, it was chiseled into rock over 75,000 years ago. Owing to the surrounding landscape and position, Josephine Flood was compelled to state that "I am going to be so bold as to suggest that it may derive from a time when terrestrial crocodiles and humans actually co-existed in South Australia, although the youngest crocodiles found so far date to more than 75,000 at Cuddie Springs."[17] According to the principles of the Dreamtime, this animal could never be carved into rock unless it was a natural and permanent part of that region in distant times. That is the Law and cannot be questioned; the image of an animal cannot be painted or etched at any location, unless it is found within that tribal estate.

Granted, all three sites only just exceed the most adventurous estimates relating to African entry into Australia, but in each case the location and distance in kilometers from any hypothetical entry point runs into four figures. Yet the discomfort of the Out-of-Africa camp is only increased by the next six sites, which are all calculated to be older than 100,000 years and cannot be ignored. If just one of these dates is correct, then virtually everything written detailing the conventional notions of pre-history must be rewritten.

According to a challenging paper compiled by a highly respected group of scholars (Drs. Richard Fullagher, Lesley Head, and David Price), there is evidence of "artistic activity inferred from ochre"[18] use and pecking taking place sometime between 75,000 and 116,000 years ago at Jinmium, Northern Territory (NT).

Their colleagues were far less enthusiastic and with surprising speed gathered en masse in co-authoring papers repudiating the science and methodology used at Jinmium. Within two years there were two substantial papers dismissing virtually everything written and done while on-site. Nigel Spooner's response, published in 1997, was warmly accepted by advocates of the current state of inertia and was seen to have "convincingly challenged"[19] these radical claims. Apparently, the final nail in the coffin was the 1998 analysis of these results, which was conducted by ten academics of some stature. The basis of this denial was simple: "some grains have older optical ages because they received insufficient exposure to sunlight before burial."[20] Outside being on-site when the grains were buried and taking note of the prevailing wind patterns and sun's movement, we are at a loss as to how anyone can determine what happened, irrespective of whether the date this occurred was 10,000 or 100,000 years ago.

When in conversation with Original Tasmanian custodian of sacred sites and lore, Tinker Gowan, I raised the issue of dates at Jinmium. He shook his head dismissively; the antiquity was never in question according to a more ancient source of information. We were standing at the headlands at Devonport, surrounded by hundreds of rock engravings, some of which exhibit a high degree of artistic talent. Tinker waved his arm in a casual sweeping arc, motioning to all the engravings we stood amongst, then replied, "The engravings at this headland are older, much older. The style used at Jinmium was first created in Tasmania and then spread to the mainland."

Gurdup Singh was supervising the extraction of a 4,000,000 year core sample taken from the bed of Lake George (NSW), when he noted a rather perplexing increase in the concentration of charcoal from 120,000 years onwards, which would take us at least another 4,000 years further back along our retreating time line. Not only was this segment in stark contrast to the patterns repeated over the earlier 3,880,000 years, the appearance of noticeable peaks within this huge increase coincided with higher lake levels and greener vegetation. With the possibility of drought, lightning strikes, and other natural agents discarded, Singh was left with only one possibility: human involvement through firestick farming.

None have challenged the implied human interference through fire, but Richard Wright has queried the date and, according to Josephine Flood, "argues convincingly for a date of about 60,000 years ago."[21] To be honest, either estimate supports our thesis. Obviously, if Singh is right, then the Out-of-Africa theory is not. Even if Wright's 60,000 years estimate was correct, it offers little support to OAT, for Lake George is over 100 kilometers inland from the southern coast of NSW and close to 2,000 kilometers from the assumed northern points of arrival. As Africans are rightly assumed by Josephine Flood to be "beach-huggers,"[22] explanations as to how such a complex community was established in such a distant location days after Africans stepped ashore is a daunting task.

Lake Eyre is normally dry, though when the rain falls, it can become the largest inland expanse of water in Australia. It is also the place where a piece of human skull was found dated through luminescence at 135,000 years. However, just as it is with the discovery at Rottnest, the presentation of the science and paper has been followed by a deafening silence.

Of course, such apathy has never been an issue at Jinmium. There were two findings originally published, the first related to "artistic activity"[23]; the second, which suggested the possibility of an even older presence, generated still greater problems because "an antiquity was alleged of between 116,000 and 176,000 years for Aboriginal stone tools."[24] Again, the suggestion that the artifacts were actually created by Original Australians has not been questioned, but it's the doubling or tripling of the earliest entry date OAT supporters propose that is so disturbing.

The next site has the potential to exceed Jinmium's upper limit on the time line. The research was supervised by three respected archaeologists. Gurdup Singh, who was considered the expert in core extraction, along with Peter Ouwendyk and Jim Bowler, analyzed a core sample taken from the Great Barrier Reef in 1983. They had a similar finding to those made at Lake George with one exception: these academics, Jim Bowler included, shared the opinion that firestick farming by Australian original people began 185,000 years ago. Elsewhere Bowler is adamant Thorne and others are wrong in claiming a date of just over 60,000 years, but in this paper he and his colleagues are prepared to more than triple that number. Not only is the date an issue, the notion of *Homo sapiens* altering the landscape so long ago is a major problem. Nor has anyone suggested that any other hominid bar *Homo sapiens* utilized firestick farming.

More controversy followed. Spooner agreed with Thorne in proposing a vibrant settled community knowledgeable in spiritual matters was living in the middle of NSW over 60,000 years ago at Lake Mungo, but sees no merit in the possibility of the same people engraving on a rock shelter at Jinmium a little over a millennium earlier. The constant changing of dates, academic repositioning on both sides of the fence, and indifference do little to engender confidence or certainty. The issue of when and from which direction the first voyage towards or from Australia first occurred seems far from resolved. It is remotely possible that when assessing the bona fides of all nine sites, the defenders of orthodox science have correctly called heads on each toss and are right. To those who support this idea, I suggest they visit the nearest casino as soon as possible.

THE FIRST BOAT

Irrespective of which interpretation prevails, there still exists a major obstacle for those who oppose the notion that the first intercontinental and global mariners were descended from the Original Australian. As previously discussed, Graham Walsh was widely acknowledged as the foremost authority on Kimberley sites and rock art, and the first to bring to the public's attention the discovery of two boats painted on a rock wall. Crewed by twenty-three and at least twenty-nine people, respectively, and exhibiting the "high prow"[25] and design of an "ocean-going vessel,"[26] Walsh jealously guarded the actual location of these paintings. Even in lectures, which author Ian Wilson attended, he would show photographs and slides of the boats but remained steadfastly cryptic in regard to the location of the site or the tribal names of the custodians; anything, in fact, that even remotely hinted at any specific place or the identity of any Elder responsible for his information.

Walsh was an eccentric character and somewhat an authority unto himself, but didn't understand the significance of these paintings. He wrote a book and spoke extensively about the fact the boats were too sophisticated, and that some art styles (particularly Bradshaw) were too refined for the cruder artistic abilities of the Original people claiming they were "painted by non-Aborigines[sic]."[27] Walsh deduced that due to the local people's primitive state, these paintings had to have been made by a mysterious race that came for a brief stay, coated caves with paint and highly advanced plans to build sturdy boats, then snuck off leaving no legacy. Not only was this a gross underestimation of the wisdom and intelligence of indigenous people near and far, it has caused a decade of mistrust between archaeologists and local tribes, as a person familiar with the offense created has confided to me.

Nonetheless, despite Walsh's refusal to supply a morsel of information when personally asked, Wilson decided to go up to the Kimberleys and look for himself. With nothing to go by but the supervised viewing of Walsh's slides, Wilson reached the last day of his personally funded expedition none the wiser. Quite despondent, he confided to the helicopter pilot his disappointment, but soon found a compelling reason to invest an extra $60. The pilot was not only aware of, but had visited many similar Original sites containing boats. Less than an hour later, Wilson found himself standing inside a cave which also had a painting of a boat with a high prow and a decidedly Egyptian feel. Granted, the crew depicted numbered four, but Wilson could not escape the similarity to illustrations he'd seen of ancient Egyptian boats and the slides Walsh kept under lock and key. Knowing that there are many similar boats painted on cave walls, the question still remained: why? Currently indigenous Australians used nothing of similar complexity and function that Wilson was aware of, and he had assumed such advanced technology was not present when the British came, and past that point it was assumed to be no different. Of course the idea of contemplating an extended period of contact with ancient Egyptians becomes much easier, when one considers the observations made by Elkin that many of the words spoken by isolated Originals from the same region were ancient Egyptian. Clearly, if this is the case, the presence of images in Australia of large boats suited to sailing across oceans is no mystery.

And that brings us, somewhat circuitously, to the eleventh site (plus one). It is much younger, by no less than 50,000 years, but it contains evidence that original people had knowledge basic to the art of navigation, which would have been a necessity for any adventurous souls sailing across oceans. Announced at the beginning of February (2011) was the discovery of a semi-circle of "carefully arranged rocks to map the progress of the sun 10,000 years ago,"[28] which "could prove Aborigines were the first astronomers."[29] The conclusion was the culmination of "years of meticulous examination"[30] by "a group of Australia's most distinguished astro-physicists."[31] Cognizant of the far-reaching implications, it was noted this discovery "could turn history upside down and render England's famous Stonehenge an also-ran."[32] The site is referred to as "Wurdi Youang"[33] and contains a sizable "strange stone arrangement"[34] that marks "the setting sun at the solstices and equinoxes when viewed from the three prominent stones at the western apex,"[35] which the researchers claim acts as a "sundial."[36] Commonwealth Science Industrial Resource Organisation (CSIRO) astrophysicist Professor Ray Norris was adamant "this can't be done by guesswork, it required very careful measurements."[37]

If this site shows that charting the movement of celestial bodies was being carried out in Australia at least 5,000 years before anywhere else, one could reasonably posit that it was the First Australians who developed such astronomical skills first and eventually shared them with other people.

Even if we are correct in maintaining these paintings are visual records of ancient deeds and the stone semi-circle actually chronicled the sun's movement, they can be no more than circumstantial and secondary categories of evidence. Compelling and repeated as they are, all of the bones/charcoal/artifacts/engravings/paintings/stone arrangements fall short in one vital area: they cannot speak for themselves. As clearly evidenced by Walsh's mistaken musings suggesting external involvement, without a voice, the pictures and rocks are merely a backdrop. Disagreements over dates, boats, rocks, and direction, these and many other issues can only return shades of maybe.

THE FINAL WORD

And so things have stood, locked in stagnation, until now. With the primary objective of breaching an ever-increasing divide, the Ramindjeri Nation (S.A.) have introduced a new phase in their culture which they call "Wirritjin"[38] (Black-fella White-fella Dreaming). Some of the secret stories to be given to the public deal with the real truth about Original boats circumnavigating the globe and their wars with settlers before the British.

Make no mistake, the secret truths revealed by the Ramindjeri and many others were passed on from generation to generation, but unlike the tales spread by rumors, gossip, and idle chatter, each word was treasured and carefully memorized. Many confuse the conquest, enslavement, and heroics of the past as the norm. They are mistaken; contrary to the path taken on all other populated continents, where armies roamed across the countryside claiming ownership of other lands, goods, and chattels, which invariably led on to the revisions and omissions of myth and history, Australia stood apart and faithful to the principles of the Dreaming. No tribe could steal their neighbors' land, Dreaming stories, possessions, or dignity; each tribal estate was protected in perpetuity from any form of conquest. As such, the local myths and history were ALWAYS kept under the custodianship of the people of that land. The bond between people, spirit, and country was forged in the Dreaming and remained intact until the British invasion. With no outside contaminating influences active and any addition or revision to the oral accounts being utterly beyond the capacity of any initiate allowed the right to listen to the ancient mysteries that belong to their land, their history and mythology has retained its integrity.

There is an old adage that has never been challenged: truth is the first casualty of war. That being the case, it is not illogical to assume the reverse applies, and lies are the first casualty of peace. If so, and within Australia before 1788 there was never issued a proclamation of war, this is the only continent on the planet whose history is authentic and was guarded by people who believed lying was a cardinal sin. Under these conditions, picking which version of the ancient past is truthful is child's play.

CHAPTER 5

THE FIRST RELIGION

It has always been our intention to walk both sides of the divide of science and religion. Both are merely human constructs that provide reason and narrative. It should never be forgotten, that until perhaps 3,500 years ago, there were no texts or accounts devoted solely to history, and more often than not, details of the past were enmeshed in the religious books and oral myths of each culture. Neither interpretation can claim perfection, nor should a religious text be held in any less regard than Uranium Series Dating. The small sampling of archaeology and science previously discussed indicates a global situation and an Australian point of departure, but outside the fact that travels were made, what then took place is beyond the reach of scholars and has been stolen, forgotten, or poorly understood.

Although one of many lands that has had contact with the Great Southern Land, Egypt's interaction with Australia is extensive and forms a long chapter in any comprehensive review of archaeology, history, or oral accounts. However, for the purposes of this chapter we will ignore the empirical evidence and focus upon the religious impact of the Dreaming throughout Egypt and the Middle East. Historically, this region has seldom enjoyed a state of harmony since the beginnings of "civilization" but has rather been unsettled and embroiled in disputes with neighbors near and far. Within such a divisive climate, the teachings and inspiration of the Dreaming have endured many ordeals and zealous censorship. Through competitive farming practices, the pressures of increasing population, and a regime predicated upon fostering a male hierarchy, much has been lost. Regardless there are, in our opinion, two beacons that stand above the separation between the divine and institutions of earthly power: the Isiac religion and authentic Christian/Gnostic scriptures.

Obviously, in other localities, Indigenous religions, Celtic and Pagan faiths, and many mystical groups remained faithful to the spirit of the Dreaming, but within this region it would appear Isiac and Gnostic philosophy were, at their essence, rewordings of the First Religion. Our comparisons to Gnostic lore and scriptures also provide some reasons why Christianity splintered, and raise issues of unfinished business that demand resolution.

As a yardstick, when assessing the authenticity of all off-shoots of the Dreaming, we have identified eight fundamental principles which must be present before we can establish any connection between a particular faith and the First Religion.

1. Equality between genders.

2. Equality with all species and "products of nature."[1]

3. Reincarnation of a tri-partite soul—"soul,"[2] "spirit,"[3] and "mind"[4] with distinct roles given to each element during incarnation.

4. Enlightening revelations and mystical wisdom supplied by the Serpent.

5. Shared ancient myths sourced from Dreaming stories—humanity fashioned out of the soil, Adam and Eve, the Fall, Tree of Knowledge, the Serpent, Garden of Eden, the Flood, etc.

6. The presence of secret teachings and ascending levels of initiation.

7. The importance and validation of visions, extended periods of introspective silence, and walkabouts.

8. Commitment to faithfully replicate original teachings as passed on through Elders/sacred texts/oral traditions without amendments.

The first two requirements stand above all other guidelines, and are absolutely crucial prerequisites woven into the very fabric of every traditional Original society and, if lacking, consigns whatever remains to a history of men behaving badly.

THE FEMININE FIRST

As an essential first principle, there has to exist within genuine Gnostic scriptures an unconditional commitment to the equality of sexes. As such, the belief that Mary Magdalene was Jesus's partner in matrimony and philosophy is consistent and obligatory. Once her husband was crucified, she became the custodian of the secret teachings they preached. In esoteric circles, it was accepted that Mary, not Peter, was the first Apostle. According to Jesus, Mary's "heart is raised to the kingdom of heaven more than all thy brethren"[5] and she alone "shalt inherit the whole Light-kingdom."[6] Whether or not the Gnostic veneration of feminine qualities was its greatest strength and eventual "Achilles heel" is a moot point, but it is undeniable Gnostic accounts place Mary as no less than first amongst equals. In the *Gospel of Philip*, there is a concern jointly raised by some of the male Apostles that points to an obvious disparity in mystical vision.

The Savior "loved her more than all the disciples and used to kiss her often on her [mouth]" . . . "They said to him, 'Why do you love her more than all of us?' The Savior answered and said to them, 'Why do I not love you like her?'"[7]

His question was rhetorical and never meant to receive a reply, and what follows is outside the comprehension and vision of the other disciples. Jesus's love, made obvious through his constant displays of physical affection, is certainly not solely driven by testosterone; there is a deeper element to his devotion based upon an appreciation of Mary's talent and degree of enlightenment. In this regard she is exceptional.

"When a blind man and one who sees are both together in darkness, they are no different from one another. When the light comes, then he who sees will see the light, and he who is blind will remain in darkness."[8]

Such vision is Mary's alone. It is quite obvious that Jesus feels Mary can "see the light,"[9] whereas everyone else assembled is still afflicted by varying degrees of blindness. Her superiority is repeatedly attested to in a variety of Gnostic accounts. In the *Gospel of Thomas*, Mary asks Jesus, "What are your followers like?"[10] His response carries no admonishment or reminder she overstepped her station through omission. If anything, his opening observation, where he likens the others to "little children,"[11] has the feel of parents discussing the welfare of their offspring.

The sense of Mary's elevation above the male disciples reappears throughout *Dialogue of the Saviour*, where she primarily makes revelatory statements and comments, while Matthew and Thomas ask questions. But on one occasion Mary breaches the final divide, where not only does she nominate what should be revealed, she also proclaims that this wisdom is exclusively the province of Jesus and Mary. The other two men are excluded from her sermon; her continued use of plural pronouns indicates the equality between Jesus and Mary.

"Mary said, '. . . I will speak to the Lord concerning the mystery of truth: In this we have taken our stand, and to the cosmic we are transparent.'"[12]

Mary is declaring that this mystery is already understood. She is not seeking wisdom from Jesus, but revealing certitude to the two Apostles. Mary was responsible for raising this weighty topic, confident in her insight, and her stance is presented as representative of Jesus and herself. The next verse only emphasizes the disparity in enlightenment amongst the chosen three, as it portrays Thomas in earnest discussion with Matthew deciding what they will ask Jesus when he returns. We can assume whatever private dealings took place after Mary's statement of purpose, both men were not part of that mystical revelation.

The existence of this partnership in ministry is clearly evident in the Gnostic scripture, *Pistis Sophia*. It has the distinct "feel" of a husband and wife in discussion at the kitchen table. So much so, that when Mary Salome interrupts a sequence of twenty-seven consecutive questions asked by Mary Magdalene, Jesus's consort could not contain herself and answered the question on behalf of Jesus. Jesus not only encouraged but praised Mary for acting as an independent interlocutor. Of the sixty-nine questions or declarations made by the twelve male and seven female Apostles, Mary Magdalene is responsible for fifty-eight. When assessing the depth and insight of the declarations and queries made which exhibit a higher appreciation of the esoteric, there are twenty questions that reach this loftier category. Whether initiating a theme yet to be discussed, expounding in greater detail upon an issue previously raised by Jesus, admonishing "my brethren have heard and let go"[13] or bringing Jesus's exposition on one area to a close, on every occasion Mary Magdalene is either speaking or directing the agenda. She was acting like a *Dirranghan* (a female adept of esoteric teaching).

Such a radical acknowledgment of equality was out of kilter with the times and offensive to some within the ranks of Jesus's chosen few. In the Gospel of Thomas, Peter made it clear all women are offensive and utterly unworthy in his eyes. "Simon Peter said to them, 'Let Mary leave us, for women are not worthy of life.'"[14] From the moment Josiah decreed Ashera, Yahweh's feminine equal, be banished from all court records, around 620 BC,[15] the status of women began an inevitable descent that led to them being treated as a lesser species. That being the case: while the elevation of Mary to a level above all other males was offensive to the status quo of the day, it was not without an ancient precedent.

Diane Bell spent considerable time living with Original women adept in traditional lore. She soon discovered that one poorly misunderstood ritual, assumed by all white male anthropologists to be solely a male ceremony, was never one which excluded women's involvement. The final cut in the circumcision ritual, with a stone knife, could only begin after a woman of standing whispered into the ear of the Elder holding the blade, the name of the woman the young man will marry. That night, before any secret men's business is revealed, the women sneak up and take the initiate aside and repeat the same mantra, hour after hour. "That women bore him and women will marry him."[16] The first lesson taught to the male novice, before any man spoke, was that women are no less than equal.

It is an essential lesson that began at Creation. The Dreaming story, *Djunkuwu*, is based upon the actions of the first Creation Spirits. It tells how two sisters discover that their brother stole their dilly bags (a traditional Australian bag made of native fibers) containing emblems of power and sacred ritual. The older sister took the unheard-of step of not punishing, but rewarding, this theft. She realized that women's magic was secure, this knowledge is innate, and more importantly, they have their uteruses, which do not hold the symbols, but the actual power of creation. She decided to let him keep the talismans in the hope that men would develop their weaker mystical skills.

The power of the feminine in the higher esoteric realms is a recurring theme in many Bundjalung Dreaming stories. *The Gummi Brothers* is yet another testament to the exclusivity of female mystical power. The narrative provides a detailed account of how, through navigation across the ocean, the three families, sailing from an unstated easterly destination, appeared in a "great canoe."[17] Through misfortune their grandmother was separated from her family. She used her magic to call up a storm and alert her sons to her whereabouts. The boat was capsized, and the brothers and their families barely survived and had no way of responding to the mother's magic beyond frantically swimming towards the shore. After establishing three tribal settlements, the Grandmother passed on her mystical powers and knowledge (women's business) to her daughters and granddaughters.

In another Bundjalung Confederation Dreaming story *The Dirranghan Who Lived in a Cave*,[18] an old naked woman acts as judge and executioner when deciding whether a male had earned the right to be called a Clever-fella. Just getting to this cave at the top of the cliff face was an ordeal in itself. The teacher was an old Dirranghan of exceptional power, and each male apprentice would spend months under her tutelage. At a time deemed proper, when the Dirranghan decided her student had learned enough to take the final step, testing her apprentice's power was as easy as stepping off a rock. She offered each applicant the same choice: step off the narrow ledge and plummet or float. There was no shame, or pain, in failure. Unknown to any man given this ultimatum for the first time, if they failed in their attempt to overcome the attraction of gravity, the old woman would always intervene and cushion the fall.

After Mary Magdalene and her followers were exiled from Judea on a boat without rudder, oars, or sail, with the justifiable expectation all aboard would perish, through the intervention of miracles all arrived safely on the shores of Gaul. After establishing her esoteric ministry, Mary retired from public life and spent the rest of her days meditating in a cave on the side of an extremely steep mountain. She was naked, and it is claimed her long hair sensibly masked her nakedness, thus lessening the offense to those of more conservative morality. Any who wished to gain her counsel had to scale the treacherous incline, then wait for her to impart the wisdom of the ages.[19]

Mary Magdalene was merely acting as a Dirranghan would and no differently to how Daisy Utemorah did when she selected male Elders. She revealed to Dianne Bell how the women choose men of outstanding talent and introduce them to some "secret women's business." The hidden knowledge the women so judiciously guarded is a treasure of which very few men are worthy and highlights the status of women in traditional indigenous Australian societies.

"SAME AS ME"[20]

Whether clad in feathers, fur, scales, or skin, all parts of creation evolve from the same source. This equality between all things, irrespective of whether they be a tree, snake, or person, is a distinctive trait that is a pivotal element of the Dreaming. Understanding this primal sense of connection is the second essential element of any religion that remains faithful to its Original inspiration. Undeniably the followers of the exoteric version of Christianity assert that there is a distinction between the souls of humans and all lesser species, alleging that due to the privilege of being fashioned in "God's image" they are in an elevated category. Christianity's esoteric sister, Gnostic Christianity, is not so exclusive, stressing scripture after scripture that all forms of life share a common source and destiny.

In the *Gospel of Eve* it states, "they say that the same soul is scattered about in animals, beasts, fish, snakes, humans, trees and products of nature."[21] There is no ascending hierarchy or separation, nor are humans listed first. Moreover, the forms of life that precede humanity (snake and tree) resonate to an ancient Australian influence. Original Elder, Big Bill Neidjie, knew all forms of life are "same as me."[22] "Listen carefully, careful and this spirit e come in your feeling and you feel it . . . anyone that. I feel it . . . my body same as you . . . star, moon, tree, animal, no-matter what sort of animal. Bird or snake . . . all that animal same like us."[23] Both Eve and Bill are in total accord and, unfortunately, entirely in opposition to the doctrines of most institutionalized religions.

This matter was of such importance, Jesus spent more time expounding upon the parity of all forms of life than any other question or issue raised in *Pistis Sophia*. This scripture was set in the times after crucifixion and just before Jesus's final ascension. He pledged to "reveal . . . all things"[24] as this issue was of the highest priority. His sermon was given in response to Mary Magdalene's request that he share with them details of the beginning of creation. We suspect this issue, and the associated obligation to respect all forms of life with which we share a symbiotic relationship, is the most important lesson given to his Apostles. Requiring more than 1,500 words, the seriousness of this passage is accentuated by Jesus's promise to "hide nothing."[25] Not only did he praise Mary for the quality of her question, he alerted all disciples to "give ear"[26] to the importance of what was about to be revealed.

"Well said, Mary; thou questionest finely with thy excellent question, and thou throwest light on all things with surety and precision. Now, therefore, from now on I will hide nothing from you, but I will reveal unto you all things with surety and openness. Harken then, Mary, and give ear, all ye disciples."[27]

True to his word, and faithful to an Australian Original script, Jesus was adamant there is no difference in order or origin between all life forms. Jesus harkened back to ancient mythologies and narratives which are strongly reminiscent of the Creation myths of the Dreaming. The spirits "gathered together all matter . . . and the servitors of the sphere which is below the aeons, take it and fashion it into the souls of men and cattle and reptiles and wild-beasts and birds, and send them down into the world of mankind . . . and they become souls in this region."[28]

Jesus speaks in the plural using "they"[29] in a totally inclusive manner, insistent in refashioning the pyramid of life into one continuous circle. Beginning in the Dreaming, the interrelationship of species is as continuous as it is inclusive. Jesus, as is the case with Eve and Bill, makes no distinction and highlights a crucial bond between each soul. All of this and so much more is part of an ancient legacy that spreads across scriptures and into the opening pages of Genesis. There are many events and parables that are almost identical in plot and script to the creation myths of the original Australians. The Flood, Adam and Eve, the Tree of Knowledge, the Garden of Eden, the Golden Age, even the maintenance of a vegetarian diet until boarding the Ark during the flood, these and many other legends did not originate in the pages of the Bible or any other book.

PRE-GENESIS

In the very beginning, Biamie (the central Creation Spirit) made humans from the "dust of the ridges."[30] As stated in Chapter 2 of *Genesis*, Adam was formed out of the "dust of the ground."[31] From this metamorphosis of soul and matter, man and woman were naked and lived in harmony with nature, as it was in Australia until the British invasion.

To begin with, both the Dreaming and the Old Testament state that the Creator's original intention was for people to adopt a vegetarian diet. As such "every herb bearing seed . . . and every tree . . . to you it shall be for meat."[32] Until the waters rose and Noah built an ark, Biamie's directive that "the plants you shall eat . . . but not the animals I have created"[33] was obeyed. In Australia the same prohibition on the eating of flesh was divinely ordained, but once again the extremes of weather foiled the Creator's plan and diet. A drought, worse than any ever experienced, led to one warrior breaking this sacred covenant with Biamie by killing a kangaroo rat. "Biamie's intention for the men and animals he loved had been thwarted. The swamp oak trees sighed incessantly, the gum trees shed tears of blood, which crystallized as red gum."[34] The Original people were also subject to the devastation of a huge flood, which covered most of the land. As it was with Noah, they also had the foresight to build a "great canoe"[35] and "sailed from island to island"[36] in an attempt to rescue "any blackfellow."[37]

In the Dreaming story "First Man, First Woman," just as it was in the Garden of Eden, the first two people lived together as partners in paradise but were lacking in purpose and wisdom. In what seems an obvious parallel to the supposedly forbidden tree of knowledge, the woman is the focus of action and enlightenment. It is the woman, as is the case in many Gnostic accounts, who reveals a "sudden insight"[38] to man. Illuminated through wisdom revealed by the Serpent, she becomes aware that they too can create babies. In the Gnostic scripture, The Apocalypse of Adam, Adam held no reservations in praising Eve's spiritual expertise. As he explained to Seth, Eve "taught me a word of knowledge of the eternal god."[39] Acting in the same fashion as the Dirranghan in the cave, Eve revealed to Adam that "we were higher than the god who had created us."[40]

The First Australians also had access to "a magic tree."[41] Described as a tree which bore the "Father of All fires,"[42] it was a gift to all people and made by the Creation Spirit, Yondi. This was a sacred tree, a place where all people would gather around for a common purpose, to "light the firesticks which they took"[43] back to their tribes. Whether viewed literally, as a place where fire was shared between different tribes, or a metaphor symbolizing the inter-tribal attainment of esoteric wisdom, the parallels with the tree of knowledge in Genesis are inescapable. In both cases the tree serves the same purpose, and with the exception of the rewritten account found in the Old Testament, it is a blessed device that shines light on hidden esoteric secrets.

The reasons why Eve and Adam were banished from paradise after independently seeking out knowledge, the real purpose behind the Serpent's intervention, our ability to be "higher"[44] than the celestial beings responsible for creating humanity, along with the personal responsibility to seek out visions, go walkabout, and discover the real nature and cycle of death, are but ripple effects of the Dreaming and issues to be examined in a future chapter. All of this and so much more were the founding principles of the First Religion. Obviously throughout the globe changes occurred, but even so all hunter-gatherer societies remained faithful to the general precepts of the Dreaming and flexible enough to accommodate nuances in culture and environment. This mystical heritage of the Original Australians held fast until the advent of the plow and emergence of sedentary lifestyles at around 8,000–12,000 years ago. Once the scythe was cast, humans began farming the land, caging animals, clearing forests, and fell into open conflict with their nomadic cousins.

The farmers won the day and wrote the books. But the truth never disappeared and irony was never lost. Of all the publications in Western societies, the Bible occupies a special place. What is yet to be recognized is that despite the deletions and in spite of many revisions, all religious scriptures, and this includes Christian texts both Gnostic and orthodox, are, at their very best, second-rate copies of the First Religion: the Dreaming.

CHAPTER 6

PYRAMIDS ACROSS THE WATERS

Our brief sorties into North and South America, Japan, Malaysia, and India yield evidence of the same ancient Australian genetic and spiritual influence, but until we examine the archaeology of Africa, thus completing our coverage of the Indian-Pacific Ocean Rim, the case on behalf of ancient Original mariners and the Dreaming is incomplete. In our opinion there are two outstanding examples of cultures whose religion and social mores resonate to an Australian inspiration: the Isiac and Dogon religions. In this chapter we intend to focus solely on Egypt and the religious renaissance that occurred under the stewardship of Isis and her consort Osiris, then follow with a comparison of the religious beliefs of the Dogon and the primal philosophy of the Dreaming.

To begin at the beginning, apparently within a matter of a few centuries, from a country of typical nomads there evolved a highly sophisticated society replete with a complex religious system and a penchant for building pyramids. The reasons or inspiration have never been satisfactorily explained; however, there are references found in ancient Egyptian texts that present possibilities and a location rarely contemplated.

In opposition to the mainstream belief that there was a sudden transformation, there is a passage in the Turin Papyrus that presents a far more ancient and exotic Egyptian history. It states that "36,600 BC Rulers before the Followers of Horus started"[1] (the Followers reign began at "13,400 BC"), but doesn't give specific details as to who and from where these "rulers"[2] came. However, other "old Egyptian writings"[3] aren't so circumspect, declaring that "their civilization learnt to build the pyramids from an ancient people who once came from a great south land to the east."[4] There are only two "great south"[5] lands which are positioned east of Egypt: Antarctica and Australia.

If seeking a more specific answer, perhaps the boomerangs found in Tutankhamen's tomb may narrow the field.[6] Of itself the replication of the boomerang design could merely be coincidental, but the discovery of the bones of a wide array of Australian marsupials near the Siwa Oasis is much harder to ignore. The *Cairo Times* (1982) reported that "archaeologists working at Fayum, near the Siwa Oasis uncovered fossils of kangaroos and other Australian marsupials."[7] Outside these animals having been imported from Australia on a boat of some considerable size, there is no other logical explanation for their presence available.

Complementing the evidence for these voyages across the Indian Ocean by Original mariners is an account compiled by Reverend Dann, which was serialized by the local Far North Coast (NSW) newspaper, *The Northern Star*. So sensational were his claims, that non-Originals were in the Far North Coast of NSW over 3,000 years ago, I made personal contact with him to ascertain how he came to make such radical assertions. Armed with a statuary declaration signed by light-horsemen stationed in the Sinai Desert during WWI, he was more than willing to state his case. The document in his possession testified to the fact that these Australian troops had stumbled upon the wooden remains of many ancient ships when patrolling the shores, which were identified at a later date to be the remains of a Phoenician armada sunk during a naval battle. These soldiers, all chosen because of their bushcraft and skill in handling horses, were adamant the wrecks were built from Australian Blackbutt timber.

THE PILGRIMAGES

Also of Australian origin is a surprise find by scientists attached to the British Museum who noted the fact that from 1,000 BCE onwards, eucalyptus resin (only found in Australia) was used in Egypt when embalming the dead.[8] No doubt some would object, claiming the embalming process is uniquely Egyptian, but this belief stands in opposition to the proliferation of mummified remains found throughout the Top End of Australia. Of particular relevance in exhibiting an almost identical process of disposal was the booty stolen from Darnley Island (Torres Strait) in 1875. Behaving with customary paternalistic high-handedness, members of the Sherwood Expedition stole a mummified corpse and its accompanying funerary objects. Momentarily disregarding the dubious ethics of such desecration, it is worth noting that world renowned medical scientist, Sir Ralph Cilento, who examined the corpse, stated "the incisions and method of embalming to be the same method as those employed in Egypt in the 21st to 23rd Dynasties over 2,900 years ago."[9]

The elaborate process of mummification carried out by Original Australians involved "removing their stomach contents. Then extracted the brains by making an incision through the nostrils with a bone instrument . . . they embalmed the corpse and rowed it 2 miles westward out to sea in a canoe shaped like the 'Boat of Ra' of the Egyptians, for internment on an island of the dead."[10] As accurate and revealing as this commentary is, the parameters need reversing, simply because the "Boat of Ra"[11] was not the model for the Australian canoe but its descendent.

The connection between the two traditions is further emphasized by the startling similarity in their conception of the fate of the deceased. In the case of the First Australians, they believed that, "depending on the soul's actions the recently deceased would gain passage to the after-life (Purelko) or be devoured by a crocodile."[12] The understanding of the Ancient Egyptians was that when judged by Osiris, "if just a feather outweighed the soul's errors, the crocodile deity (Ba) consumed the fallen sinner."[13]

Not only were the wayward souls of Egypt and Australia consumed by a crocodile spirit, the coffins used before disposing of the body and soul share a rather distinctive temporary means of escape before final internment. Australian "burial coffins had a small opening, providing an opportunity for the soul to come and go using the coffin as a home-base. The Egyptians also left a small aperture in the tomb of the deceased for the individual's soul (Ka) to leave and return as it saw fit."[14]

We believe these facts go some way towards explaining the reception Professor Elkin received when making first contact with Original men of the Kimberleys in 1931. After unsuccessfully trying to communicate through the use of neighboring languages, the Elders broke the impasse. It became apparent the Elders may have been illiterate and naked, but this primitive exterior was juxtaposed against worldly knowledge that is generally only the province of academics, Freemasons, and ancient Egyptians. This highly regarded anthropologist's report detailed their extraordinary reaction: "The Professor was astounded when tribal elders greeted him with Ancient Secret Masonic hand signs. He was struck by the startling Semitic features present in the natives. He discovered the Aborigines worshipped the sun."[15] As the interaction continued, "he discovered many of the words spoken were of Egyptian origin."[16]

Many discoveries in Australia, which are of Egyptian construction or inspiration, were not uncovered through archaeological endeavor but were purely accidental. Often unearthed through the farmer's plow or laborer's shovel, the coins, tools, monuments, weapons, and personal effects recovered are as numerous as they are inconvenient.

Andrew Henderson's accidental discovery of two Egyptian coins at Barren Falls in 1910 is either an elaborate hoax or metallic proof of presence. Henderson was constructing a boundary fence when he found the two coins while digging two feet beneath the surface. They were 40mm in diameter and 7mm thick and dated at 221 BC and 204 BC. Bearing the insignia of an eagle riding on a thunderbolt, which was the symbol Ptolemy chose to represent his reign, these coins were either mischievously planted or artifacts indicative of contact. Of particular relevance is a commentary provided by Henderson, who stated that the fence line ran along an ancient Aboriginal walking track.[17]

Most assuredly these coins are not an isolated case. In the same year laborers excavating a well at Gordonvale were distracted by an unexpected discovery: a substantial amount of Egyptian jewelry, based on representations of the iconic Egyptian scarab beetle, one of which measured 90mm, along with a bronze coin dated at 28 BC.[18] This find not only broadens the region of Egyptian influence but extends the duration of their tenure to close to 200 years.

However, 200 years is merely an extremely conservative base figure. "A very small statuette of a squatting ape was found by Widgee Shire workman Mr Doug George from near Traveston crossing. Mr George picked up the rock while working near the bridge. This is also believed to be 'Thoth' in ape form."[19] "Its form was of an archaic kind, as it portrayed a part human/ape form, which was superseded by the more widely recognized ibis/human guise around 1,000 BC. When one considers no ape entered this country until after European invasion, it would be extremely difficult to convince anybody this was constructed by any local tribe."[20]

As sung by Paul Kelly and the Messengers and later by Kev Carmody, "from little things big things grow."[21] Rather than continue itemizing finds, we would prefer to change tack and move into another dimension of evidence through examining three sites which involve literally hundreds of hours in construction and narrative building. Two sites are known by critics and advocates who are worlds apart in their interpretations; the third has never been seen by any archaeologist, and if they did, they would have a great deal of trouble assembling any critique.

The hieroglyphs found near Kariong have been visited by an assortment of academics, amateur archaeologists, vandals, and inquisitive non-professionals. In a forthcoming book, we will be devoting considerable time to analyzing the origins of these phenomena and conclude that, once the obvious recent additions are discounted, some of the engravings are indeed Egyptian. Our interest is not in adding to the debate over their authenticity, but sharing with the reader what caused so much disagreement.

First found by non-Originals in the 1950s, the walls (at that time a cave) contain close to 300 glyphs, which chronicle the trials and tribulations of these ancient Egyptians. Lamenting their misfortune at being stranded in this "wretched place,"[22] the reluctant immigrants were being led by "NEFER-DJESEB, Son of KHUFU, king of Upper and Lower Egypt."[23] The scribe, who was allotted the task of recording their travels, was speaking "for his Highness, the Prince, from this wretched place . . . where we were carried by ship."[24] Referred to as "Prince"[25] and Lord, the leader of this expedition could have had royal blood. The proposal that he was "the Son of KHUFU"[26] certainly ups the stakes and, if true, magnifies the importance of this hazardous voyage.

Unfortunately, the stranded party were beset with drought, an unknown location, and infestations of marauding snakes. For reasons never stated, the Lord set off to the west for "two years."[27] The motivation for the desperate act of setting off with no real idea what lay ahead during a drought—"creeks and river beds are dry"[28]—is never engraved. As to how the party arrived in an unknown region in the first place, it is possible that they were intending to sail to a more northern part of Australia; given the evidence of mummification throughout the Top End, along with the variety of artifacts found around Cairns, the Egyptian presence in those latitudes is well attested to. A cyclone blowing in the wrong direction and their boat being forced much further south than intended are sufficient to account for their presence in more unfamiliar climes. Irrespective of how they were stranded and why, Lord Djes-eb chose to head west; when returning, he had the incredible bad luck to be "struck"[29] "twice"[30] by a "snake."[31] Despite their best efforts, including the application of "egg-yolk"[32] to revive the Lord, he died. According to the narrative on the wall, the cave was then fashioned into a crude tomb. The whole tragic affair concluded with a rather prophetic plea, asking what fate lay ahead for those still standing. As there were no further entries and no indication of interaction with the local tribes of either a hostile or friendly nature, we suspect it did not end well for all marooned in this "wretched place."[33]

PYRAMIDS IN THE BUSH

The next site has been seen by extremely few non-Originals, and the readers of this account will judge it depending on how they judge my reliability as a witness. I first became aware of this formation nearly thirty years ago when browsing through a chapter written by highly respected archaeologist Isabel McBryde. So sensational were her claims, that the constructions in question were made before Cook sailed up the east coast of Australia, I sought permission from her to examine the site in more detail. More importantly, I contacted the appropriate Original Elders and arranged to be taken on-site to be introduced to the land and guardian spirit by a person of their choosing.

Acceding to the Elders' wishes, much of what was seen, measured, and theorized cannot be revealed, but owing to McBryde's earlier brief visit, what I am at liberty to disclose will serve our purpose.

McBryde's proposed pre-Cook construction was based upon the size of a Red Carrabeen tree growing on top of an extensive man-made formation that can rightly be called a road. The forestry workers who escorted McBryde into this dense forest were all of the opinion the tree was over 200 years old, which places the date of germination at no less than 1760. The road was constructed on possibly the steepest slope in this National Park, by rocks either shaped by metal blade, as claimed by McBryde, or collected because of their suitability to their intended purpose. The road measured a little over 100 yards according to McBryde, but she did concede the severity of incline and denseness of vegetation was such that she did not venture far. She was adamant that many of the rocks of this huge construction near the Red Carrabeen were formed into rectangles by metal. The road had a uniform width (1.5 meters), obvious camber, and protective walls above and below the road to assist in drainage and stability. McBryde did not believe it could be the work of Original people. Undoubtedly there is no known structure even remotely similar elsewhere in Australia, and she is correct in assuming a foreign inspiration, but remiss in not looking further up the slope and behind the big tree.

I shouldn't be too critical; perhaps it was our good fortune to approach the track from the top of the ridge. As we began our descent, we were at least 100 meters above the segment of road examined by McBryde, and barely 10 metres from the top, we stumbled onto the remains of a road, badly eroded at both edges but still measuring 20 odd meters. What stood out was the surviving archway, which spanned a small, dry gully. We continued scaling down and across to the north, passing two more sections of stone pathway, both of about 10 metres in length, until reaching the section of road with which McBryde was familiar.

What struck us was how well preserved this large construction was, but equally, this was the least severe slope on the mountain. Although I was prepared, it was still quite a shock to see this construction so far from any signs of white-fella civilization, obviously fashioned for some activity requiring an extensive system of roads that spanned hundreds of meters. The Red Carrabeen growing over the track was indeed the largest I had ever seen, and the date of 200 years seemed conservative. The day was spent measuring and forming estimations on the time taken and number of rocks used in this section (which was in the thousands). We also decided to investigate past the point McBryde assumed the track finished. Another 30 meters on, and the road reappeared then disappeared under the roots of a Brush Box with a girth of 8.6 meters. Exiting out the other side the road continued another 20 meters then fell away into a creek which was still running in fairly dry conditions.

As revealing and unexpected as this extra, hitherto unseen, section was, what immediately caught my eye was the flat plateau measuring 10 by 5 meters. As out of sync with the topography of this steep slope as this man-made construction was, the stone pyramid positioned in the middle of this flat ledge was something that came right out of left field and some. Two meters in height, with four bases all measuring approximately 2.5 meters, there were thousands of small rocks stacked together to form an extremely precise pyramid.

I have since been informed by Doug McPherson, who was in conversation with the last fully initiated male of this region, Elder Lyle Roberts, that this location was used by Original men for a "rite of passage."[34] Not only were sacred ceremonies conducted on-site, Elders have also informed me there are other stone pyramids of similar dimensions which delineate tribal boundaries. The pyramid exists, as does a network of roads, but as to why this road straddles such a steep slope, there are rumors. Of all the possibilities, the one that does seem to have merit is the talk of mining. Irrespective of the motivation for building the road and pyramid, and whether mining or some other activity took place, the major participants were not indigenous. But undoubtedly, although they were not the instigators of this project, it could not have occurred without their approval.

A PYRAMID IN THE ROAD

Three hundred kilometers up the road, 5 kilometers outside Gympie, is a pyramid of much larger dimensions which occupies over one hectare. Consisting of six steps, the lower four are 10 meters wide, the fifth measures 5 meters and the highest is 2 meters across. It has been estimated "4,709 tonnes of rock"[35] were collected to create this pyramid. First noticed in the local area in the 1870s, it was appropriately named the "old ruins complex." At that stage the land wasn't owned, and the locals seized the opportunity and removed tonnes of sandstone blocks to use in buildings, fireplaces, and roads. Originally there were five statues erected around the complex; four were stolen and the fifth was salvaged by the Gympie Historical Society.

Of course, the academics see things differently. When scholars from the University of Queensland were challenged as to why they exhibited utter contempt for this site, their reply is as symptomatic as it is "par for the course." They stated they had "no intention do any form of investigation into the site"[36] as it "might give credibility to something which is impossible."[37] They claim this site is merely a terraced vineyard created by unknown Italian farmers (which is obviously accepted by the relevant authorities responsible for the proposal to bulldoze the pyramid to make way for a road).

However, a search of the records from 1892 onwards shows solely Anglo-Saxon names. Considered the least suitable land for agriculture and situated on the worst possible aspect for grape-growing, this proposal is decidedly feeble. In what does stand in direct opposition to such a notion, Greg Jeffreys discovered deposits of slag, "two were iron bars about 30mm wide by 10mm thick by about 200mm long."[38] In what only multiplies the chasm between the two explanations, researchers associated with the Dhamurian Society are adamant the slag is a by-product of an "ancient furnacing method called a bloomery."[39] This crude smelting process hasn't been used anywhere for more than 400 years.

As to what this all means, any explanation must be prefaced with an admission that outside the real potential that the First Australians sailed to Egypt, and at a later stage Egyptians sailed to Australia, everything else is, depending on perspective, either a mystery or unworthy of investigation. In every other case, any theory or apparent deviation from accepted versions of history we have proposed has been firmly entrenched in facts supplemented by Elders' advice or Dreaming stories, but on this occasion any explanation detailing what this all means relies upon some extensive reading between the lines.

With a reign of over 23,000 years before the "Followers"[40] referred to in the Turin Papyrus took up the reins, the "Rulers"[41] would have encouraged a nomadic lifestyle with a premium on spiritually connecting with the spirits of their land. There is a sense of separation in that the "Rulers"[42] stand above the "Followers."[43] Comfortable in their teachings and the ability of local priests of both genders to take up and adapt the mystical principles of the Dreaming, we suspect the Australian Originals were responsible for inaugurating the "Reign of the Gods" and handed over stewardship at 13,400 BC, with the expectation there was no longer a need to return. It would seem even the best laid plans can go astray, and at around 5,000 years ago it was decided the "Followers"[44] had lost their way, and one final visit was made, which was possibly the last time Australian Originals sailed abroad.

Times were changing, and many societies had abandoned a nomadic lifestyle in preference to farming and living in large settlements. In an attempt to adapt to changing realities, an emissary was sent from Australia to re-establish and modify the tenets of the Dreaming. Her name was Isis, and her brief was to recalibrate Egyptian teachings and religion, thus finding a compromise for a sedentary society that had abandoned a hunter-gatherer lifestyle. She is noted as being black in all historical accounts, but what is relevant is that there is no record of where she came from. If from a neighboring country, surely there would be some mention of reciprocal arrangements and political relations between the participating countries. Instead, there is nothing concrete to indicate any place of residence, but once her reign with Osiris began, there are some interesting similarities hinting at a distant southern location.

She, along with Osiris, instituted a dramatic change in religious direction and worship, so much so, Robert Lawlor correctly noted that "the Egyptian religious practices, zoomorphic pantheon of Gods, concepts of life and rebirth, sorcery, magic and medicine all have their origins in the primal culture of the First Day."[45] As it was and still is in Australia, the women are the innate possessors of magic and creation, and it is for this reason that Isis was the sole custodian of the sacred Shaft of Tet. Reputed to overcome the laws of science as we know them, this mystical device opened pathways to the Divine.

It all comes down to a series of unlikely coincidences or a shared Australian inspiration and stewardship.

CHAPTER 7

DOGON DREAMING

Jung believed the images stored in our unconscious and found in our dreams have been with us since the beginning of time and have similar meanings for all people . . . I believe the unconscious shared with the Nummo may be associated with the dreamtime [sic] talked about by the Australian Aborigines.[1]

—Shannon Dorey

Without doubt this chapter is a task approached without enthusiasm and has been undertaken mostly though a sense of obligation to a gentleman who has been of great assistance in our research. If not for John McGrath's research and prompting, I suspect we would have never considered even hinting at Alien involvement, nor would we entertain raising the subject of Sumerian Gods resembling fish. Extraterrestrial presence is a topic every Elder has raised, and one we deliberately pushed aside for fear of losing academic credibility. But as the years passed where not one accepted scholar would dare consider an Original version of anything, we realized we have no credibility, so with nothing to lose, here is another example of the truth the Elders insist upon, this one with a decidedly otherworldly twist.

Quite recently, when we were delivering a presentation and responding to questions, a member of the audience raised the issue of Aliens, insisting Original Elders he'd met swore they existed. Until that moment, our approach had always been to veer way from such delicate matters, but on this occasion our reply was prefaced with supporting quotes from Original Elders. Within seconds, we had completely lost one lady sitting in the front row. Her arms were folded with a frown etched into her forehead. She voiced her disappointment in that, until that fateful utterance, we had relied upon facts and logic and won her approval, but from that point on, her arms remained locked and everything we said before and after was dismissed with indignation; this talk of flying saucers got in the way of the science supported by Original history, culture, and philosophy and was a distraction best left alone. Having noted that this is a reaction which is not uncommon, it is with the greatest reluctance we begin this comparison. However, the fact that both the Dogon and the original people of Australia have been long aware of constellations, planets, and orbital paths only recently confirmed by telescope raises important questions that deserve a response.

The subject of extensive research, many books, and even more unanswered questions, the Dogon appear to be acting (in partnership with followers of Isis and Osiris) as African custodians of an ancient lore, and have often been referred to as "keepers of the truth."[2] Unlike nearly all of their neighbors who succumbed to agriculture, crusades, and inquisition, the Dogon of Mali held fast to their ancient roots. Through maintaining a strict adherence to their oral myths and teachings, and due to the apparent impoverishment of their tribal estate, they were "so isolated from the rest of the world that it was only in the 1930's that contact began with Europeans."[3] This separation, both through internal preference and outside disinterest, gives credence to the belief that of all the African tribal groups living a semi-nomadic lifestyle, which obviously excludes Egypt, only the Dogon can rightly lay claim to being bearers of the most ancient religious traditions.

With the Egyptian Empire in disarray, Mark Anthony and some prominent Egyptian priests fled across the Sahara and made their way south until they reached Dogon tribal lands, where they sought sanctuary. Obviously this wasn't the first time contact had occurred, and perhaps goes some way towards explaining the shared reverence held by both religions towards Sirius. John McGrath is of the opinion the Egyptian priests decided to share "their astronomical knowledge,"[4] as an act of appreciation "for their hospitality."[5]

Having accepted that the Dogon are custodians of the oldest form of religion in Africa, many commentators have fallen into the trap of reversing the roles of bestower and receiver. They have assumed that Africa is the place where modern humans first appeared and this pattern of precedence is repeated from then on, which is only reconfirmed when stating that "traces of it [Dogon religion] are found in many ancient religions."[6] We would suggest that the underlying ancient Australian influence, so evident in their myths and rituals, is an inconvenient and largely unconsidered truth.

The first systematic attempt to record some aspects of Dogon history occurred in 1946. Two French anthropologists Marcel Griaule and Germaine Dieterlen won the trust of Dogon Elder, Ogotemmeli, and it was through this liaison news of their culture and ceremonies spread throughout the world.

Shannon Dorey's article honors the words of both Original Australian and Dogon Elders, and its main title "The Dreamtime & the Dogon" is well chosen to indicate the order of influence. The similarities between the Dreaming and Dogon religious beliefs are so numerous and consistent it defies logic to suggest anything other than a shared heritage if not a direct influence. The real question at play really doesn't relate to whether, but how this connection that spans continents came about. To itemize all the similarities between the Dreaming and Dogon religious beliefs is a Herculean task deserving of a thick book. However, as we are limited to the confines of one chapter, it is sufficient to our purposes to present six points of convergence. A comparison of the mutual understandings of reincarnation, the Serpent, circumcision, astronomical knowledge, the enigmatic Bradshaw paintings of the Kimberley Region (WA), and the cross-continental implications discovered within a Walpiri (NT) painting of a chromosome "ladder"[7] all bear witness to many rarely discussed aspects of Original culture and history.

THE "GREAT BLACK SHAPES"[8]

We have previously examined the antiquity and breadth of Original astronomical wisdom. Of particular relevance to any study of the amazing celestial secrets kept by the Dogon are certain astronomical objects of interest to the First Australians. Establishing the precedence of their knowledge through an understanding dating back "over 30,000 years,"[9] the Original astronomers were above all focused upon the "great dark shapes"[10] formed between constellations and stars. Their knowledge of the stars and cyclical progress was an invaluable asset used by ancient Original navigators as they set sail from Australia, voyaging throughout the Pacific and Indian Oceans.

The depth and antiquity of Original knowledge of the movement and alignment of the stars and planets are displayed in the existence of extremely ancient stone constructions revealed publicly in 2013. These sites offer absolute proof that knowledge of every form of astronomical investigation began in Australia, tens of thousands of years ago.

The Dogon were aware of the unseen heavenly creations, thus explaining why "they told the French anthropologists Marcel Griaule and Germaine Dieterlen about a red dwarf star in the Sirius star system which was only discovered by modern astronomers Daniel Benest and J. L. Duvent in 1995."[11] The Dogon also spoke of its companion "the white dwarf star Sirius B. This star is invisible to the naked eye and so difficult to observe even through the telescope that no photos were taken of it until 1970."[12] They were aware of quite specific details in regard to the character of the twin stars, correctly declaring Sirius B to be "heavy, small and white."[13]

Not only did the Dogon retain distant knowledge of constellations that can never be explained through any conventional thinking, the rings of Saturn and four main moons of Jupiter did not escape their attention. Despite the fact that the possession of knowledge of such a refined nature is supposed to be incompatible with the Dogon's state of technological development, these modern-day truths are yesterday's news for them and contained within an oral tradition that reaches back into the distant past, and, we believe, ultimately to the Dreaming.

All of this knowledge and much more was not acquired through the use of sophisticated devices or a dedication to arduous and exacting studies; their understanding of distant and close realms was given to the Dogon, and the myths and rituals pertaining to the activities of their Gods were imported into their culture. Dogon oral rendition is consistent in attributing the acquisition of their esoteric knowledge to communications with Celestial Beings they called the "Nummo,"[14] who gifted them with these divine revelations.

SERPENT DREAMING

As it was in the Dreaming and countless early legends of genesis, the Gods took on the form of the serpent and were active agents in the Dogon's creation and enlightenment. The details provided by Ogotemmeli are so much in sync with Australian accounts it caught us a little unawares and a touch annoyed I hadn't taken a little more time when John raised the subject earlier. Whether describing the physical features of the Serpent (Nummo), its place of residence and immortality, there is nothing in contradiction; they both seem to be singing their own interpretation of the same sacred song of old.

"According to the Dogon, the Nummo were fish-like amphibious beings who spent more time in water than on land. While they were on the land they moved like serpents on their long, thin, bodies ... they were identified with the sacred feminine. They were perceived as being immortal, that is, when they died and were reborn, they were able to remember their previous existence. 'The Dogon elder [sic] described life and death for the Nummo as being similar to a snake shedding its skin.'"[15]

The conception of the origins and the location of these extraterrestrial beings and the desire to record into rock their deeds are common to both Dogon and Original Australian cultures, but the earliest examples of these shared traditions are found in the Great

Southern Land, and it is not unreasonable to suppose that they were originally exported from there.

Professor Alfred Radcliffe-Brown was a British anthropologist who spent decades on-site with traditional original people in Australia. In particular he focused on the collection of various myths detailing the deeds and motivations of the Serpent. Through his extensive study of the religious beliefs of the First Australians, much hidden knowledge was first revealed to outsiders. Brown was responsible for coining the oft-used, and quite accurate, phrase "Rainbow Serpent."[16] His comparison of a variety of Serpent mythologies in Australia led him to state that "many Australian aboriginal [sic] groups shared variations of a common myth telling of an unusually powerful, creative and often dangerous snake or serpent of enormous size who was associated with rainbows, rain, rivers, and deep waterholes, and descended from a larger being visible as a dark streak in the Milky Way."[17]

Consistent in their interstellar interest of the darker regions of our galaxy, Original Australian astronomers looked to distant horizons and the shapes created by the void when seeking out the birthplace of the Serpents.

The Dogon can also locate the position of the "star of the Milky Way"[18] from which the Serpent/Nummo originated.

In regard to where the Dogon got their knowledge from and Dorey's contention that it derives from extraterrestrials, it is intriguing to note that that the Dogon describe the Milky Way as resembling "a bulging funeral urn."[19] Scientists have only recently confirmed that when viewed from the side, our galaxy shows "the central bulge of the universe."[20] The question is raised, who has a perspective on our galaxy viewed from the side? Certainly not the Dogon or any other terrestrial race.

Irrespective of where an Australian Dreaming story originated, the Serpent's abode is invariably associated with or based in the water. "The words 'water' and 'Nummo' were used interchangeably."[21] The Nummo's skin was predominantly green, but had the capacity to "at times have all the colors of the rainbow."[22] The similarities between the two beings extend well beyond their hue. According to Ogotem-meli, the Dogon Creation Spirits "also had horns or casques on their heads"[23] with "an ear of millet in a long crack protruding from the Serpent's skull."[24]

According to rock-art expert George Chaloupka, there is a consistency of form throughout Australia. He identified the repeated pattern of "a snake-like body, curved horse-like heads, at least two types of tails (pointed or spiked), and an assortment of plant and animal appendages, including wispy tendrils and ear-like projections."[25]

Of particular relevance is that "the horse was also a symbol of the Nummo,"[26] which becomes even more problematic when surveying the unique fauna of the Australian landscape. There never has been any animal roaming the countryside that vaguely resembled a horse; in fact the only comparison offered by the First Australians when confronted by this exotic beast was to call them large possums. This may seem a poor choice for comparison, as these animals are obviously very different on so many levels but, in a land of small marsupials and kangaroos, there was nothing better on offer to use as a comparison. The incorporation of the features of an exotic beast not native to Australia into this sacred icon suggests knowledge and contact unsuspected by all but the initiated.

Undeniably, the Serpent occupies a dominant role in every ancient religion but when ascribing a source, the place from which this myth originated, there is only one possible candidate if we are to consider the oldest known example in the world. The present-day respected authority on the Rainbow Serpent, George Chaloupka, has worked on an art site in Arnhem Land in the Northern Territory which contains the oldest painting "in the world"[27] of a Rainbow Serpent dated between "9,000 and 7,000 years."[28] According to Josephine Flood, this "would make the Rainbow Serpent myth the longest continuing religious belief documented in the world."[29] As expected, as with so many other firsts, this universal myth, in its form and message, has its roots in Australia. As is the norm, over the years and throughout the lands, the details and powers of these Creation Spirits have been given a local expression in distant locations and have accommodated a variety other influences. But there is one African location where the people refused to deviate from their past, and continued to maintain the integrity of their oral traditions and Original wisdom.

An ability invariably shared by the adepts of both religions is the utterly unscientific talent of shape-shifting. Stepping well outside the province of any accepted field of physics, there were Dogon Shamans and Australian Clever-fellas/women who could change their material appearance. In both instances, the Rainbow Serpent/Nummo was intimately connected with this transformation. What must be pointed out is that any argument over whether or not these deeds actually occurred as described is irrelevant. That they are virtually identical stories though separated by over 10,000 kilometers of ocean and land is the issue that cannot be resolved if hamstrung by convention.

There is an account found within an Original Murrinh-path Dreaming story that is strongly "reminiscent of the Dogon religion."[30] So important is this myth it was part of a key tribal ritual and "is performed in Murrinh-patha ceremonies to initiate young men into manhood."[31]

"A woman, *Mutjinga* (the 'Old Woman'), was in charge of young children, but instead of watching out for them during their parent's absence, she swallowed them and tried to escape as a giant snake. The people followed her, spearing her and removing the undigested children from her body.

"Within the myth and in its performance, young, unadorned children must first be swallowed by an Ancestral Being (who transforms into a giant snake) then regurgitated before they are able to be accepted as young adults with all the rights and privileges of young men."[32]

The responsibilities conferred upon those initiated into adulthood, with the Serpent's assistance, are an honor and provide a pathway to enlightenment. Without initiation, no matter what age the male is, he will never become a man and will always remain a child.

The old woman's ability to shape-shift and take on the form of the serpent isn't exclusive to one Australian tribe. The Nummo also had the ability to transform, and the myth as revealed by Ogotem-meli to Marcel Griaule, with the exception of a minor variation of subplot and gender, is an identical account. Both stories serve the same underlying purpose.

"The myth of the Bina Tire, ancestors of Ogotemmeli's family, which originated in the Sodamma quarter of Upper Ogol, was a good example of this. The ancestor, when he became an old man, was in the habit of looking after the children in his eldest son's house, while the adults were away at work. One day he changed himself into a serpent, which frightened the children. As, however, he resumed his ordinary appearance when the men came back from work, the whole thing was put down to childish fantasies. But it happened again, and one day the eldest son, returning unexpectedly from the fields, surprised the old man in his transformation . . ."[33]

As it is with all traditional Original religions, the Dogon believed in reincarnation. They, along with their Serpentine Gods, went through the same process of birth and decay, but there was one distinguishing difference in that "when they died and were reborn, they were able to remember their previous existence."[34]

This retention of the knowledge of previous incarnations, along with an assortment of mystical powers and perceptions, were gifts from the Gods, but there was a "price to pay" for such knowledge. Initiation, in all its diverse forms, was an essential part of the educative process, and none was more important than the ceremony that unlocked the door to the adult world. The complex mythology and rituals associated with circumcision are a pivotal event in Dogon society and turning point in which every male was given the opportunity to fulfill his destiny. They see circumcision as a symbolic act that leads to the removal of a "second soul."[35]

The Nummo swallow the foreskin of the young man, which they refer to as "the jackal's foreskin,"[36] thus creating the potential for the initiate to become "the perfect combination of Nummo and human."[37]

This process is identical to the circumcision ceremony held by the Murngin tribe and witnessed by Joseph Campbell. "When a little boy of the Murngin tribe is about to be circumcised, he is told by his fathers and the old men, "the Great Father Snake smells your foreskin; he is calling for it."[38] The implication being, what he smells he will surely eat then swallow, as is the case with all successful Dogon/Murngin initiates.

However, after this consumption, the process is incomplete. The Dogon believed the supreme Nummo deity/leader (revered as the "Master of Speech"[39]) symbolically swallows then regurgitates an enlightened human named Lebe. This offers yet another parallel with Original myth, for the Murngin Dreaming story is quite explicit in how the children are swallowed, reclaimed then "renewed."[40]

Not only do the oral accounts of the Dogon and Murngin resonate to the same themes, the cave walls of the Kimberleys seem to be drawn directly out of Dogon ritual, dance, and dress. Referred to as Bradshaw Art, these extremely distinctive and intricate figures replete with "elongated headdress, pubic 'aprons', armlets and tassels"[41] have all the hallmarks of Dogon dancers who do actually wear all the appendages depicted on many Australian cave walls. With dates of over 20,000 years attributed to these fine pieces of art, running through to 9,000-year-old paintings of Serpents, all found in Australia then carefully reproduced in Mali, the likelihood of any convincing explanation being forthcoming, other than an Australian migration abroad, is scant.

So dramatic is the artistic sophistication of style, some have mistakenly assumed these paintings, and those of "massive"[42] "ocean-going boats"[43] which could be up to 50,000 years old, were the product of an unknown and far more advanced race which most probably came from Africa. Offensive claims like these were popularized by Graham Walsh, who alleged "there was a long hiatus between the Bradshaw and Wandjina traditions,"[44] which gave ample time to account for this earlier intrusion from, and return to, Africa. Owing to Walsh's popularity and the book he published proposing this exotic origin, relations between academics and traditional Original custodians took a marked turn for the worse. Although obviously in error in his conclusions, Walsh's observations are worthwhile in one respect alone, they confirm that there must be a connection between the so-called Bradshaw figures and the Dogon art that so resembles them.

The recurring problem when any examination of Dogon culture is undertaken, as it is with Sumerian religion, relates to the other-world identity of their Gods and the genetic manipulation claimed to have been carried out by them in order to create humanity. Irrespective of the merits of arguments offered in support of external intervention, the mere mention of extraterrestrial involvement creates a reflex reaction in many academic circles. What needs to be appreciated is that the entire issue is irrelevant to our argument. Our interest here lies in what beliefs were exported from Australia; what may have taken place before departure necessitates another chapter. Whether these celestial beings are described metaphorically or literally in either or both countries is open to question, but there is a commonality and connection that both spans continents and opens up distant perspectives.

Anthropologist Jimmy Narby was able to extend his vision much further when "viewing a painting of the Rainbow Snake drawn by Aborigines of the Walbiri tribe."[45] Of course his "evidence" is purely subjective, but that is the inherent nature of the Serpent.

"I looked at it more closely and saw two things. All around the serpent there were sorts of chromosomes, in their upside down 'U' shape, and underneath it there was a kind of ladder. I rubbed my eyes, telling myself that I had to be imagining connections, but I could not get the ladder or the chromosomes to look like anything else. Several weeks later I learned that U shaped chromosomes were in anaphase one of the stages of cellular duplications which is the central mechanism of the reproduction of life and the first image of the zigzag snakes looks strikingly like chromosomes in the 'early anaphase,' at the beginning of the same process."[46]

If seeking an icon that best represents the serpent, the original Creation Being which has always been synonymous with the beginning of life, chromosomes would be a logical choice. Of course Narby's intuitive response is totally inconclusive and offers no shred of scientifically verifiable evidence, but his rarely taken approach may be desperately needed. Of utmost importance, in his introduction he states, "I looked at it more closely,"[47] simply because the application of "second sight" is a mandatory though rarely employed recourse for those seeking esoteric knowledge. Almost invariably when academics wander on-site, they think they already know what to look for and, therefore, all new evidence merely reinforces preconceptions already formed off-site. Narby "looked ... more closely"[48] but did so without the clutter of the left hemisphere. He had no understanding or theory to champion before entering the cave, acting solely as a recipient. The wisdom gained could only be offered to those prepared to seek with their eyes wide open and soul at the helm.

As to whether the serpent's form, which does have a ladder structure within and is surrounded by U-shaped objects in "anaphase,"[49] is a cryptic chromosomal map or a figment of imagination can never be proven or refuted. Equally, even though we are awash in a sea of circumstantial evidence supporting an Original presence and involvement in the spiritual heritage of the Mali, as yet no Original bones have been recovered there. However, the reverse should also apply in that there are no African artifacts, bones, or genes found in Australia, to support the oft-asserted theory of Africans migrating by boat to the Great Southern Land. Therein lies the real dilemma, facts and truths in support of an Australian genesis abound but require a skill which is sadly becoming a lost art: to look "more closely."[50]

"OUR ALIEN CREATORS"[51]

We also have chosen to employ Narby's intuitive approach when investigating the mystical legacy of the Original people. The Dogon deserve no less, and the facts we have briefly discussed warrant much more recognition than has been forthcoming. As mentioned earlier, the inertia verges on scholarly paralysis whenever the issue of the Dogon and their alleged extraterrestrial Gods is raised. Consider, for instance, the title given to an article on the Dogon written by Shannon Dorey:

THE DREAMTIME AND THE DOGON.
OUR ALIEN CREATORS.

It begins with a plausible contention and adds a more daring suggestion as an addendum, no doubt because many have been unable or unwilling to separate Dorey's arguments into their distinct components. Opening with facts, the comparison of the Dogon Elder's quotes and Dreaming stories presents a compelling case in support of a shared inspiration. However, it is more than likely that very few academics will get to these because they won't bother to read past the three words of the subheading introducing the extremely contentious issue of Alien involvement. No matter how convincing Dorey's argument may be in other regards, her material is condemned due to guilt by association with this pariah of the academic world.

The clouding of two separate issues summarized by this title and its sub will obscure the vision of many, but even so, there are facts and repeated coincidences that point toward conclusions outside the limitations of current mainstream thought. How can any traditional authority on human pre-history find a rational way of explaining how the Dogon were aware of the location and characteristics of stars not even known of when their stories were recorded? Without a telescope or written records and reliant solely on oral tradition, how is it possible that the Dogon knew Saturn had rings or Jupiter had four main moons? These astronomical facts were recorded in 1946. It took another fifty years before the astronomers of today, using the most expensive equipment and advanced computers, were able to confirm what the Dogon already knew centuries ago.

These facts demand to be "looked at more closely" and need to be prefaced with the realization that there are some aspects to this case that point beyond the limitations of commonly accepted academic assumptions. There is no conventional theory that comes close to explaining how the Dogon knew of the location and distinguishing features of these distant celestial bodies. That is a fact, everything related to Saturn, Jupiter, and the twin stars of Sirius should not be known by primitive Africans bereft of telescopes, books, and universities. There is no earthly reason that could account for these facts being known . . . but they were.

Explanations accounting for this celestial knowledge, outside those that push the limits well beyond this solar system, are scarcer than hen's teeth. True to a response encountered in many similar instances, it seems any inconvenient archaeology that does momentarily raise questions and eyebrows is destined to receive equal servings of apathy and avoidance. We would much prefer to offer a solid response assembled by defenders of the current academic status quo, anything that may shed light on these apparent anomalies would balance the books. But alas, there is one meager offering defending the traditional model and an abundance of theories on the other, of which many readers of publications like *New Dawn* would be familiar.

The case for negative and jaded was presented by Alan Baker in his book *The Enigmas of History*. Devoting a chapter to "Sirius—The Mysteries of the Dog Star,"[52] he tries to balance his overview by first presenting a variety of accounts more than sympathetic to John McGrath's position, managing to locate one publication that debunks these nonsensical interpretations laced with Alien mischief. Baker is of the opinion James Olberg's clinical analysis of information recently imported into Dogon oral mythology, compounded by the omission of what ought to be known, "calmly demolishes the argument for extra-terrestrial intervention by beings from Sirius."[53]

This contention is as perplexing as it is inconsistent, and could only be accepted if we replace aliens with the Tardis. It defies logic for Baker to endorse Olberg's rationalization that the Dogon "could have learned of European Sirius lore in the 1920s from traders"[54] and "amateur astronomers."[55]

How could this be? "European Sirius lore"[56] during the 1920s was confined to Sirius A. The discovery of Sirius B was decades in the future, and it was most definitely unknown when the French recorded the words of four Dogon Elders. The only fact that is not in dispute is that knowledge of the smaller companion star was first detected in the night sky with the assistance of the most sophisticated optics in the 1970s.

How then did the Dogon know, not only of its existence but, as Baker concedes, that it was "heavier than all the iron of the earth,"[57] and that Sirius A orbits B "every 50 years,"[58] and is "100,000 times fainter than Sirius A."[59]

The second criticism raised by Olberg relates to the original anthropological report and the apparent errors in science. Elders' statements testifying to a belief that Jupiter had four moons and Saturn marked the outer limit of our solar system were enough for Olberg to discredit the bona fides of these so-called benevolent Aliens. He deduces this incomplete celestial chart seriously questions the actual existence of such incompetent celestial navigators. However, before judging these "errors" as cardinal astronomical sins of omission, it is necessary to address the cultural sensibilities not observed and offense caused in the gathering of this sacred knowledge. Marcel Griaule's daughter, Genevieve Calame-Griaule, was adamant her father's research was flawed in that he did not observe the relevant steps essential for acquiring deeper knowledge. If so, who is to say that other teachings describing the solar system and beyond were not deliberately kept secret because Griaule and Dieterlen did not observe Dogon protocol? Undeniably the two men came with the best intentions and tried to act honorably. However, it is an unwarranted assumption that anything not spoken of indicates ignorance rather than reticence. It may merely be part of a much larger story rightly withheld from uninitiated researchers from outside the tribe.

Regardless of such speculations, even Olberg was forced to admit, in one of his more candid moments, that the knowledge of Sirius B was indeed a mystery. The arguments cobbled together are illogical and more importantly, an insult to the Dogon people and their cultural heritage. To suggest, as Olberg did, that the Dogon would so quickly inculcate into their sacred lore the astronomical musings of people not of their tribe, for the express purpose of manufacturing a "colorful embellishment"[60] is as patronizing as it is ill-informed. The religious myths held sacred by the Dogon are an integrated union of religion, ethics, and history, not a piece of fiction to be added to and deleted as the editor sees fit. Such a sacred legacy is passed on, generation after generation, faithfully preserving the essence of who the Dogon are, from where they descended, and the identity of those who guided them. Importing another story compromises the purity of the paradigm and taints its sacredness. This didn't happen; the Elders gave up a small taster, an introductory first step, and to this day, unless the notion of Alien involvement is applied, nothing makes sense.

Before presenting John McGrath's somewhat cosmic take on who, why, and what, we will first begin by taking up residence near, but not on, the fence. We are convinced the conventional explanations are at best extremely weak and suspect John is most probably right but, if he is not, it makes no difference to our theory. From our standpoint, what he claims is in keeping with the facts and is no way opposed to anything we have proposed, and it is for that reason, and in appreciation for John's assistance, we will now present a version of ancient events that can comfortably accommodate an illiterate group of nomads possessing intimate knowledge of star systems and planets unseen by the eye.

For John McGrath, the crucial part of the Dogon narrative relates to the description of their principal God, Nummo. Described as "fish-like amphibian beings"[61] who "spent most of their time submerged in water,"[62] he noted striking similarities to the physical appearance of the deities of the Sumerian creation myths. John is of the opinion, the Gods of Sumerian and Dogon genesis accounts are based on the same intervention from afar. In either case, these beings "came from the Dog Star constellation Sirius."[63] The spaceship, which he feels was not the only alien craft carrying other life forms who chose to become involved with the development and affairs of the hominids of earth, crashed "in the Persian Gulf and sank to the sea-floor."[64] These semi-aquatic beings, who originated from a planet orbiting the Sirius twin-stars which was primarily "of a very swampy terrain,"[65] chose to settle within "the reedy swamps of the Tigris and Euphrates estuary"[66] that bordered "the Persia Gulf."[67]

The reasons for coming, according to John, are twofold. As to whether their motivations were altruistic or less enlightened is debatable and an avenue others have explored in far greater detail. Equally, in both endeavors they may have had the assistance of other extraterrestrial visitors in both mining for gold and "experimenting with *Homo erectus* by adding their own genes to make *Homo sapiens*."[68] What can't be determined is whether this was done as a liberating experience or to build up a stock of more intelligent workers. Regardless, this potential genetic manipulation by Aliens sits comfortably within our theory. As discussed earlier, both Alan Wilson and Rebecca Cann proposed *Homo erectus* entered the Australian continent 400,000 years ago then evolved "free from competition."[69] It is possible that they escaped the genetic engineering, acting as a control group of naturally occurring *Homo sapiens*. Either way, neither Wilson, Cann, nor any other adventurous academic has explained what inherent factor or external agent was responsible for this transformation, just that it occurred.

The Dogon knowledge of the heavens is unaccounted for by the mainstream academic understanding of the past. Furthermore, if not originally extraterrestrial, then the earthly source of this wisdom remains a mystery, if it is not Ancient Australia. Irrespective of whether Dorey's predictions as to where the Serpent Gods originated from are correct, she wisely decided to balance her supposition with a truth. It was for this reason her paper begins by walking with the spirits and announcing itself as "The Dreamtime & the Dogon"[70] in that particular order. Our main interest is in determining which community of *Homo sapiens* were the anointed custodians and first "keepers of the truth."[71] Determining the earthly trail and human agents responsible for spreading the Serpent's teachings is a realistic goal hardly less confronting than determining some more outré inspiration from the stars. Moreover, once one factors in such evidence as the presence of Original bones in America and Malaysia dated at over 10,000 years old, Original genes within the DNA code of some full-descent Ainu and Dravidian people, the bones of Australian animals recovered at Siwa Oasis, Egypt, and the earliest paintings of a Rainbow Serpent and depictions of "massive"[72] "ocean-going boats"[73] discovered in Australia, deciding whether Mali or Australia is first among equals becomes a much easier task.

Of course, there can never be a definitive answer as to what happened tens of thousands years ago, just degrees of doubt, but what can be stated with confidence is that the Dogon of Mali are one part of a global story that began in the Dreaming.

In an earlier chapter we began an investigation into the nine central tenets of the Dreaming. These principles have inspired many religious traditions and all truly spiritual attempts to grapple with the Divine. To fully appreciate this ever-present Australian connection, which is so clearly evident in both Isiac and Dogon religion, we will examine the other six principles of the Dreaming in our next chapter.

CHAPTER 8

THE FIRST RELIGION (PART 2)

Having established the existence of a substantial body of evidence in archaeology, science, and history supporting an Original presence in ancient world affairs, we would like to bring to a close some unfinished business. Irrespective of whether fully or partially convinced, or not all, this small sampling of empirical evidence can only be, at best, half the story. Before passing final judgement, we believe the consistency in repetition of the central tenets of the Dreaming found within many religious teachings throughout the world deserves serious consideration. Ancient religious accounts shouldn't be casually dismissed. Until quite recent times there were no books devoted solely to the topic of history; in nearly every case, stories of people and remarkable events were first chronicled in religious texts or oral traditions. It now seems an appropriate time to revisit and complete our investigation into how the Dreaming influenced and inspired all other spiritual paths. We proposed that there are nine guiding principles apparent when comparing Original spiritual beliefs to other religions, of which Christian Gnosticism was our first "port of call," but six of the principles mentioned in our earlier chapter, "The First Religion," were listed but never discussed.

In each case, and those already raised, the same pattern prevails. Irrespective of what aspect of the Divine is compared, the source was the Australian Original people and their mystical foundation, the Dreaming.

Of the nine fundamental aspects that indicate a common mystical heritage with the Dreaming, there is no need for further discussion of the principles of gender equality and parity with "products of nature" or the many shared first stories detailing creation. Our focus in this chapter is solely upon those aspects not yet covered. The six topics to be addressed, albeit briefly, which complete our comparative study, include reincarnation, the Serpent, secret teachings and initiation, visions and going walkabout, personal responsibility in creating an individual's destiny/karma, and lastly, Egypt. The inclusion of Egypt is only relevant to the Middle Eastern strand of the Dreaming, simply because Gnosticism was sourced from Egypt, via Australia. If studying the Original spiritual effects in India, Egypt would have no impact or relevance.

The first fresh subject we will now turn to is reincarnation. Whether rudimentary or sophisticated, an understanding of rebirth is a central element integral to any belief stemming from the Dreaming. Whether there is a belief in two or three components that make up the reincarnated person is of undeniable importance, but in the broadest terms, as long as the principle of returning to earth to remediate poor choices in previous lives dominates, that is of itself sufficient.

THE RETURNING BRIEF

However, there is a huge difference in the understanding of the mechanics of this process of spiritual return. The Dreaming, along with more authentic hybrids, which include some animist faiths, the Isiac religion, and Christian Gnosticism, are prime examples of a sophisticated perception of motion and rest. These religions hold fast to the separation of each individual into three elements. That which is dependent upon the material plane for its existence is referred to in the *Gospel of Mary* as the mind, *ka* in *Isiac* religion, and recognized simply as the flesh by the First Australians. In its simplest terms, it is the chosen earthly vehicle used during each incarnation.

The next two elements are of a mystical origin and independent of time and decay. The "soul,"[1] as understood in the Dreaming and *Gospel of Mary*, is the unique essence of each individual, which reincarnates after each death into a new body. The ancient Egyptians called this spiritual force "ka." However, in most after-life accounts, irrespective of whether they describe one mortal existence or many, the body and soul represent the complete picture. But there is another passenger in this journey. Whether referred to as "ba" in Isiac mythology or the "spirit"[2] by Mary, this element of mystical identity was first revealed in the Dreaming. As sophisticated as the replications evidenced in Christian Gnosticism and Isiac lore are, they still fall short at the very highest level. They share the conception of each soul reincarnating lifetime upon lifetime, often making the same mistakes, but they are in error in assuming that every "spirit" or "ba" automatically merges into a universal soul upon death. The teachings of the Dreaming shed light on the last step taken by enlightened individuals when they die. Some great Original "spirits" remain beside sacred sites and become bound to the landscape and power of that specific location. So powerful has their spirit become, it serves no purpose to merge into the collective when the wisdom learned could best serve in a more direct fashion. Conversely, those who are embittered by revenge and attached to ego can become shackled to a place and often fall to baser emotions.

THE SACRED SERPENT

Once set on the path towards redemption through rebirth, there is still the need to seek signposts and direction and, in this regard, the Serpent, the major Creation Spirit in the Dreaming, fulfills the preeminent role of guide. Not only is the Serpent a crucial component of the Dreaming, it is, at face value, a rather perplexing central character found in virtually every religion. Before addressing the similarities, what needs to be factored into any analysis of the Serpent's pivotal role in the genesis of humanity is why, of all the creatures on the planet, a reptile of reputedly low intelligence was chosen to orchestrate humanity's liberation or disgrace? These reptiles do not strike an empathetic chord with the great majority of people but, on the contrary, elicit a reflex reaction of fear from most. Distinguished German anthropologist, Dr. Hermann Klaatsch, noted the case against this reptile and the contradictions involved in its role in spiritual life, as well as the strong potential its spiritual significance originated in Australia.

"The case of the serpent, which has a quite special position in religion up to the highest stage, is conspicuous even in the Biblical narrative of creation. Every thoughtful person must ask how this rather repulsive creature comes to occupy this position in the venerable story of Eden, and is even made to thwart the plans of the Creator. In harmony with the whole mosaic nature of the early part of *Genesis* we may see it as a fragment of some older religion; and, as we know that the serpent was a sort of divinity, even in such civilized religions as the Babylonians ... throughout the whole of Australia, in particular, there are stories told of a great serpent, living in the water in lonely places."[3]

A creature of unrivaled adulation, the role of the Serpent from the very beginning is a central character and agent found within the very core of Original spirituality. If, as Klaatsch proposes, the serpent is a "fragment of some older religion,"[4] which he suspects originated in Australia then spread throughout the globe and into so many creation myths, it should be a simple process to compare and order.

The fervent veneration the Christian Gnostics offered the sacred serpent would not disappoint any original Australian custodian of traditional lore. The Ophites, the sect many believe was the source from which all forms of Christian Gnosticism evolved, literally placed their snakes on pedestals. Snakes were allowed to freely slither amongst the devotees in the most holy of their rituals, which culminated in the actual kissing of the serpents on the mouth. They stated that they "venerate the serpent because it is the cause of gnosis"[5] and that it "taught men and women the complete knowledge of the mysteries from on high."[6]

Of course the affront this reverent attitude caused advocates of the exoteric strand of Christianity was only heightened by their diametrically opposed interpretations of the Serpent's role. The Ophites, as did all Gnostic offshoots, believed "the Mother, by means of the Serpent"[7] instructed Eve and Adam in the "knowledge of the

Virtue which is above all things."[8] However, many theologians and exoteric scholars regard the serpent as a subversive trespasser who was in league with the devil. Jean Doresse identifies this Gnostic reptilian "perversity of character"[9] as a fatal flaw in Gnostic theology and, of itself, ample justification for its suppression. Although we do not support Doresse's vilification of the Serpent nor his sense of revulsion toward it, we must concede that he was partially correct in assuming this myth was "sourced in Oriental philosophy."[10]

In America the same tradition is apparent. Legend has it that "the first inhabitants of Yucatan were the 'People of the Serpent.'"[11] If we accept, as seems increasingly likely, that the pre-Clovis *Homo sapiens sapiens* Americans were of Original Australian stock, the bestowal of this title is entirely apt. As in Australia, the reptile occupies an unrivaled position in American myths and rituals. The legendary redeemer Quetzalcoatl, who came from and returned to an unknown land by boat, along with "Votan, the great civilizer . . . both sharing the same symbol of the Snake."[12] The icon and totem of Izamna, the Mayan God of Healing, was a snake. And so the pattern continues, whether considering India, America, the Middle East, or any other location, the reverence of the snake is spread throughout the world over the ages.

THE SACRED PATH

Another mystical thread, which binds together all genuine interpretations of the Dreaming, relates to a hierarchical set of secret teachings and sacred objects. To earn the right to learn secret business, men and women among the First Australians undertook a huge array of extremely trying physical tests and deprivations. They had to complete their esoteric rite of passage through fortitude and the ability to conquer considerable pain. Faithful to the same general sentiment, Gnostic rituals were much more a feat of memory and application than an ascending series of increasingly painful rituals. Gnostic teachings catered for those seeking higher truths and personal salvation. It was originally intended that there be two complementary strands of Christianity, with the esoteric scriptures devoted to sacred intuitive wisdom being restricted in circulation and public exposure.

The replication and infiltration of many sacred Original ceremonies throughout the world are far greater than most would suspect, and the examination of one of the most painful forms of initiation, circumcision, merely confirms how strongly the Dreaming influenced all other religions. Once a young Original apprentice successfully copes with his first cut, whether circumcision, tooth avulsion, scarification, etc., some knowledge is shared and a few simple sacred truths are spoken of, but much more is hidden and will remain so until the seeker can pass further tests and take more cuts.

For young Original men circumcision with a stone knife was a common practice. The absence of any cut was a major obstacle for the ancient Greeks when trying to convince Egyptian priests to share just a small snippet of their history and culture. No matter how impassioned the plea, the Greek scholars and scientists were uncircumcised and regarded as children. As it was in Australia, Egyptian priests were unequivocal in demanding their foreskin had to be removed with a stone knife before any secret and distant historical knowledge could be revealed. Only after a supplicant agreed to circumcision did Egyptian priests agree to open their books and discussion.

And so this ancient Original initiation spread throughout the region. All of Noah's male offspring were also initiated in the same primitive fashion. Even though metal was freely available and firmly established as part of their technology, according to Noah's wishes his male children were circumcised with a stone knife. From that recorded act, Christianity, and many other religions, adopted circumcision as a rite of passage, but as is often the case it was a hollow copy and a lost opportunity. Initiated when extremely young, within days of birth, what can then be revealed to an infant that sleeps, smiles, cries, and can't understand one syllable uttered by priest or Clever-fella/woman? When in puberty, the pain is intensified and the young man is ready, willing, and able to listen and learn. The initiate understands this ritual marks the beginning of the next stage of his life and ascension in adulthood; the three-day-old child realizes very little and can absorb nothing of significance beyond experiencing the base emotions.

Associated with ascending secret business is a wide variety of talismans and secret objects. In the Dreaming story *Djankuwu*, once the older sister realized their brother had stolen a dilly bag full of sacred objects, she chose to let the theft go unpunished. For the first time men had devices to assist in reaching the spiritual heights the women were naturally positioned for. Sacred objects, holy sites, and initiatory wisdom that are outside the comprehension of Western science have been in existence since the Dreaming began. Crystals and magic chords used by Wee-uns and Clever-fellas are reported to have powers of magic and enlightenment and are the forerunners of such artifacts as Isis's rod, the Staff of Tet, which was reported to be able to bend the laws of science. Sites like Stonehenge and a multitude of objects like the Holy Grail are in the same tradition.

The emperor Constantine supervised the censorship and restructuring of Christianity into a religious dictatorship. His legacy still stands today: cathedrals, buildings, holy books, men in control, and all under the jurisdiction of the self-proclaimed Thirteenth Apostle of Jesus. His self-ordained task was to decide what Jesus wanted in print, then rule by force as a divine proxy, and therein lay the dilemma and inevitable conflict.

The proscriptive exoteric message is in stark contrast to the introspective explorations of Gnosticism. The Gnostic disdain for regime and absolutes, when coupled with the insistence that the kingdom is found "within," focuses on a perspective where each soul is unique and capable of direct communion with the divine. There can be no cathedral, priest, or set of commandments; in fact, the only firm directives issued by Jesus related almost entirely to what should be avoided.

Not only are Mary and Jesus antagonistic to the concept of an institution, they made it clear they had no interest in any form of prescribed prayer, diet, fasting, or financial donation to any church. If fortunate enough to have more money than is needed, one is obliged to negotiate a financial loss through finding, "someone from whom you will not get it back."[13] Adding to this list of cardinal restrictions, Jesus was quite specific when proclaiming to his disciples in the *Gospel of Mary* to relinquish their urge to impose rituals and create structure.

"His followers asked him and said to him, 'Do you want us to fast? How should we pray? Should we give to charity? What diet should we observe?'

"Jesus said, 'Do not lie, and do not do what you hate, because all things are disclosed before heaven. For there is nothing hidden that will not be revealed, and there is nothing covered that will remain undisclosed.'"[14]

GOING 'WALKABOUT'

To neither lie nor intrude with poor intentions into another's affairs sums up the recommended behavior and temptations to be avoided. But as to deciding what should be said and done, that is why each soul is blessed with free will. Poor performances in past incarnations necessitate future lessons and disappointments and owing to the truth of reincarnation and personal responsibility, there is no book or sermon given by any third party that can exceed the status of merely one opinion. It is this sense of personal responsibility and the need to engage in constant self-reflection which must be at the core of any faith that has kept its ancient mystical heritage intact. There can be no supreme leader, no holy building, or anointed book that stands above the flock. Realization comes from within; everything else is background noise. Under these parameters, not only what is declared, but also the style of delivery and spaces in between are just as important.

Original people all reserve time for reflective silence and intuition, an opportunity to commune with the spirits and the pulse of the land, on a sabbatical sojourn referred to as 'walkabout.' In *Pistis Sophia* Mary Magdalene's demeanor is typical of an Original Australian Elder. This is revealed in a section the importance of which is emphasized by it being the longest reply offered to Jesus's Apostles in this text. The manner in which Mary takes a lengthy pause before asking her question is a perfect sixty-minute "snapshot" of traditional Original ways.

"It came to pass then, when Mary had heard the Savior say these words, that she gazed fixedly into the air for the space of an hour. She said 'My Lord, give commandment unto me to speak in openness.'"[15]

Jesus's response to her request to speak, after one hour of contributing nothing, seems very reminiscent of Original Australian meditative practice. To commend someone and place them above all mortals in advance, with no words or participation to base an exaltation of this scope upon, is a bold vote of confidence. Jesus knew that after one hour of continuous consultation with the kingdom of the Father, whatever Mary was about to proclaim was divinely sanctioned and deserving of the highest praise.

"Mary, thou blessed one, whom I will perfect in all mysteries of those of the height, discourse in openness, thou, whose heart is raised to the kingdom of heaven more than all my brethren."[16]

His carte-blanche promise to reveal everything after spending one hour on an internal "walkabout" is as warranted as it is Original. As expected Mary's question/observation met Jesus's expectations, so much so that he praised her for being the "fullness of fullness and the perfection of all perfections."[17]

There are two options available when determining where the inspiration behind Gnostic Christianity was sourced, it either evolved spontaneously and completely out of Jesus's ministry, or came from an older scripture or tradition. To our knowledge there isn't a commentator on either "side of the fence" who makes claim to Gnosticism being sourced from anywhere other than Egypt. There is a consensus amongst Biblical and religious scholars of all persuasions, that all esoteric faiths in the Middle East and some parts of Europe were preceded and inspired by the teachings of Isis and Osiris. Both Osiris and Jesus were born in a cave or animal shelter, turned water into wine, were betrayed by a trusted disciple, crucified on a cross, and resurrected three days later in the presence of their consorts who were renowned for wearing red. In this fashion, the narrative echoes throughout the region. Our interest is not so much centered on the conventional Egypt-out scenario, but it is much more an issue of into-Egypt.

CHAPTER 9

A NATION OF ADAMS AND EVES

"I hope the English annals will never be stained with shedding innocent blood. What are we to think of men who have already notoriously forfeited the friendship of their own countrymen, and then denied the benefit of our lives and society, now going to colonize with guns, etc? Will they benefit at all a race of people who are content with the spot nature has allotted them; whose wants are few and whose virtue, perhaps, exceeds our capacity for thinking; they go quite naked, so did Adam and Eve in Paradise."[1]

The most important understanding cultivated that was an essential element of every Original mystical medicine chest was an apparently naïve approach towards death that verged on being cavalier. The familiarity and comfort that traditional Original people possessed in regard to their own mortality were at odds with a European society that barely acknowledged the existence of such a solemn, awkward truth, let alone eagerly embraced it as a blessing.

Merely one of many steps within the revolving circle of life, each death is laden with unlimited potential according to Original Australian spiritual beliefs, but for many outside that culture, the dilemma of mortality has confounded both philosophers and religions. Regarded as merely another initiation, death was and still is an essential tool for every Clever-fella/woman to absorb and master.

In the Dreaming, death is a means to an end, and the opportunity to be reborn, in body and soul, into the tribe and land. A report, collated by Professor Elkin, still remains the only authenticated testimony that describes the events involved in the "making" of a Clever-fella. However, any attempt at understanding this gift must be prefaced by the realization that history, as portrayed in the Dreaming, is eternally vigilant in observing the truth, but its narration is often cryptic in expression. Elkin correctly claimed that this "account, the only one, of medicine men and their making, has been published"[2] with the willing assistance of *Unagarinyin* (*Ngarinjin*) Elder David Mowaldjali. This Elder's standing and knowledge of traditional lore is immense, and he was quite open in sharing previously unpublished details of what happens when the seeker makes contact with "rai"[3] ("spirits of the dead"[4]).

The rai are very discerning about the type of person they consider eligible, accepting only someone who is "discreet, poised, and firm; he is not a troublemaker but has good sense and is trusted by the rai."[5] The initiate was considered suitable for elevation to the status of "Clever" if they were deemed to be of good character, possessed of appropriate knowledge and wore the insignia of scars which displays a proper degree of initiation. The process of further initiation, however, involved a test of fortitude and excursion into mystical realms that no one could be guaranteed to pass or even survive.

"There they cut him up and hung up his insides (intestines, heart, lungs, liver, kidneys). His body is dead, but his soul remains there, and on the order of the rai to look steadily at the part hanging up, he recognizes them. His body is put over a hot earth-oven, with magic cooking stones in it, and covered with paper-bark. The rai then replace his insides and close up the flesh. He is told that he can henceforth travel in the air like a bird or under the ground like a goanna (Australian lizard). Actually he is sleeping in one place while travelling in the mind, for 'his spirit became many.'"[6]

The suggestion that enlightenment can only be gained through dismemberment is a challenging proposition at every conceivable level. Yet examination of the phenomenon suggests to us that the death may be at times physical as well as symbolic, even if dismemberment is not actual.

There are countless records of many who have died, crossed the divide, and claimed to have entered a tunnel of white light where they were welcomed by guardian spirits. In what seems a common observation, the deceased person then acquires some form of startling insight, invariably lost by degrees when returning to their inanimate body. Although the specifics are lost, there still exists the imprint of a divine revelation of life-changing importance within the individual. Their claim that a sense of absolute fulfillment overwhelmed their disconnected soul, before being reluctantly pulled back, is in itself convincing in its consistency.

The concept of near-death experiences is no longer the province of New Age bookshops and clairvoyants. The phenomenon is so widely reported and has been of such enduring interest that "doctors at twenty-five UK and US hospitals will study 1,500 survivors to see if people with no heartbeat or brain activity can have "out of body" experiences.[7] So incessant have these reports of near-death crossings been, up to "10–20% of people who are revived back to life report some activity of the mind."[8] The three-year program, which began on September 17, 2007 and was coordinated by Dr. Sam Parnia, focuses on this phenomenon that resonates with an experience central to an ancient ceremony that began in Australia.

"If you can demonstrate that consciousness continues after death switches off, it allows for the possibility that the consciousness is a separate entity."[9]

What these scientists are investigating, is whether or not "consciousness,"[10] which is the essence of the individual, is an independent quality that is mystical in complexion and eternal in conception. If so, the flesh is a temporary vehicle for the soul to inhabit then discard before reincarnating into another body. Of course, when consulting Original mythology, the necessity of separating body and soul to reach enlightenment had been realized and embraced as an integral part of the circle of life and death for tens of thousands of years.

The out-of-body experiences Dr. Parnia intends to investigate are random and uncoordinated in every case, not part of the regime of the Dreaming. However, those who do return retain a vague sense of the significance of what has occurred. Even though many of the results of this brief experience can never be proven, these people seem more complete, cognizant of a greater picture and the intent of the

Creator, and at ease with life and its uncertainties. In many cases there is a tangible transformation in attitude and soul that leads to the formation of a more content and peaceful person.

Whether on an operating table or cave floor, the "death"[11] David Mowaldjali spoke of is transformational, but in his case the knowledge remains intact, and the contact with the Dreaming is constant. Once permanently straddling this divide, there are no questions or limitations. This type of transformation goes beyond the bounds of "normal reality": "Mowaldjali does not say whether all the foregoing experience was in a single dream or trance or in several."[12]

Before making any attempt to fathom what was symbolic, real, or both, there is a need to first appreciate the commonality of this fatal prerequisite to seeking out the spirits, and the underlying truths shared irrespective of tribal affiliations. Quite simply, to be an Original Clever-fella/woman, death has to be welcomed and experienced, there can be no other way. If this dramatic event is misunderstood or feared, the magic rope which is awarded to those aspiring to gain these supernatural powers has no home to reconnect with and will remain hidden.

When R. H. Matthews was in contact with tribes from northwestern NSW early in the twentieth century, he was compiling a list of the rituals practiced when striving to become clever, and noted that the protocols involved "varied little from generation to generation."[13]

To that we would add with absolute certainty, the most significant ceremonies varied little in form from tribe to tribe. Somewhere secret and sacred within their tribal estate, the postulant "was then taken to an isolated place to sleep; it was haunted by spirits who, he was told, would take out his kidney fat or perhaps the whole of his insides and give him a fresh lot."[14] Their beliefs are identical to those of the *Unagarinyin* (WA) who believe "Unngud had killed"[15] the person before imparting enlightenment. While the *Bundjalung* also insist the body is merely a fleshy device which is opened up, whereupon many sacred "things"[16] are placed inside the organs before it is sealed. This consistency spans the continent, and their sensational claim is simple and repeated without exception or modification: the higher levels of esoteric wisdom can only be initially accessed through an actual death that is confirmed by the pulse stopping.

Many a patient on an operating table or victim in an accident, where the person was revived after being clinically dead, have made claims about what occurred next that has much in common with the ritualized dismemberment of an Original Clever-person. In both cases the resurrection of the temporarily dead was due to the actions of a "doctor," who through knowledge of their sciences reunited a body and soul. The outcome of one procedure is haphazard for it is only designed to restore physical life, not to revitalize the spirit. In Western medicine any such psychic phenomena is considered a quaint side effect of curiosity value at best. However, the ancient path, traveled under the guidance of the spirits and a mentor who has already walked in this direction offers so much more, as the souls who are allowed to return retain the knowledge revealed. Those on the table or trapped in the wreckage may bring back snippets of wisdom and vague recollections. However, the contact made by Original Australian men and women was neither so random nor accidental— they willingly volunteered to die for the cause. To be found worthy of receiving honors of this magnitude, the seeker has to be remade and reborn, armed with esoteric knowledge and magic that serves one function: to assist the tribe to live within the boundaries and blessings bequeathed in the Dreaming.

What needs to be made clear is that during such a dramatic initiation, a reunion with the living was not an automatic progression, but a privilege offered to many postulants, certainly not all. Some fled in terror when confronted, while others bravely stood refusing to flinch: the outcome was always dependent upon the hidden intentions and character of the applicant. If lacking in honor, perhaps a touch vain or even worse, selfish, their "death" was always laden with the distinct potential of a one-way ticket.

It is undeniable "the near-death rituals in the name of Baiame, the All-Father, were so severe that many Aboriginal men actually died as a result of them."[17]

For any critic who still steadfastly maintains this ordeal where the body is torn apart then dies, is purely symbolic or a sign of ignorance, an interview conducted by Professor T. G. H. Strenlow with one of the "last of the Western Aranda medicine men,"[18] contradicts this assumption. This Clever-fella was a person of impeccable character and dignity, and most assuredly "a man of high degree,"[19] who had no understanding of what a lie was or is. Despite all the qualifications and meritorious deeds he brought to his initiation, the real and present danger was so tangible and overwhelming when standing at this sacred site, he admitted to "once running away in terror from the grimness of the ordeal."[20] If purely a figment of his imagination, a psychological anomaly, how would fleeing from a geographic location assist if this horror was imaginary? Of one truth this Elder was resolute, once leaving the site the danger immediately disappeared, and only when he summoned up his courage by making his way back to this sacred place, did the fear, and his inner-battle, return.

And so these esoteric expeditions between the realms have continued since the Dreaming began. The manner in which this occurred is truthful within the settings of their culture and tribal estates. However, by its very nature the Dreaming is often too mystical and nebulous to be defined by anything other than metaphors and parables, but on this specific occasion there are no vagaries to interpret. The only means of accessing this level of esoteric contact was to first lay your life down and willingly hand your fate over to a spirit, and let the fateful results fall as they may. This is a spiritual process rather than merely a brush with death though it is, also, assuredly that. Once the postulant vacates his or her body to set off on this spiritual journey, the magic chord provides a possible anchor and point of eventual return. But this is no guarantee of safety, and while in transit in the ethereal realms, the flesh is without soul or heartbeat, and if the cord is broken by the guiding spirits, that incarnation is deemed complete.

For those that do survive, their body and soul have been remade. This ceremony is crucial in establishing who possesses the wisdom to advise the tribe.

When the initiate returns as a fully ordained Clever-fella/woman, it is through "this dream or trance experience, Mowaldjali says the trainee's mind is being 'conditioned.' He is being shown in his mind what to do. And by his total experience and training he is set aside, ordained, as we might say; he becomes an expert."[21]

The death spoken of is real in every sense, while the accompanying dismemberment could be a metaphor that describes the process by which every fiber of the postulant's being is remade and reinvigorated. According to Original mythology and doctors, each organ has a spiritual allegiance which needs to be purged of all negativity. Once this is done, the individual organ can regain its pristine form so that it can relay and amplify the powers and wisdom first discovered when cast into this suspended state. If the body is allowed to remain in a spiritually polluted condition, upon returning to the flesh the messages from the Dreaming will be confused: as is the norm with a large percentage of near-death experiences. For any wishing to become "clever," their body must be made anew, the organs revitalized, sacred objects inserted, and then, if the spirits feel the novice is of exceptional character, brought back to the material realm with one task. His or her role is to act as a beacon and conduit, to throw light for those whose vision is unclear, and give inspiration and substance drawn from the Dreaming.

This ritual is not unique and many replications have been created. An account found within the Gnostic scripture, *The Secret Gospel of Mark*, detailing Jesus's raising of Lazarus from the dead, appears to be sourced directly from the same Original practice. Jesus was told that Lazarus had "died,"[22] and after some delay decides to attend to his body. As he nears the tomb, a spirit from within the tomb who was guiding Lazarus in his initiation reacts to Jesus's presence, but this occurs before the Messiah spoke or anybody announced his appearance on the scene. From inside the cave where the body of Lazarus was placed, "immediately a loud voice was heard within the tomb."[23] Once Lazarus had returned from his guided near-death experience, admittedly of an extended duration, Jesus then took over and rewarded Lazarus by "teaching him the mystery of the kingdom."[24]

The revelation of mystical teachings given secretly to Lazarus was an outcome of his successful return, wholly supervised by a spirit in the "tomb."[25] Jesus was not an active agent in orchestrating Lazarus's return to the material domain; his role is to complement the wisdom revealed by the "loud voice . . . from the tomb."[26]

The tradition and ceremonial aspects of this event were highlighted, but rarely considered, in the *Gospel of John*. When Thomas first heard of Lazarus's ceremonial death, he reaffirmed the esoteric nature of this journey into the higher realms when enviously lamenting, "Let us go, that we may die with him."[27] This sentiment is in keeping with Original expectations of the potential this deadly ritual offered those who returned. Thomas was either advocating mass suicide or the pathway towards enlightenment.

The fact that the obvious parallel between aspects of Jesus's practices and those of Original Clever ones has never been recognized highlights the reluctance, one might say *aversion*, of many Western commentators to treat Original Australian mystics on a par with those of other lands.

Granted a justifiable dread of derision, condemnation, and public ridicule may have convinced many to look elsewhere if seeking similarities, but there always exists a greater imperative that should obliterate such petty issues: to tell the truth and accept what follows.

According to Christian teachings, Jesus was exceptional and unique. In traditional Original times nothing he did was exceptional and each person had at least a little bit of "Jesus" in them, some less, some the same, and maybe, just maybe, a few even had a little bit more "Jesus" in them than even Jesus. All divinely inspired prophets tell the same story; once enlightened, there really is no hierarchy of ascending value within messages, especially so when the sermons and messengers tell different versions of the same ancient tale that began in the Dreaming.

Ignoring all evidence from every printed word, story, photograph, gene, bone and artifact, there is still more than enough that we have experienced at a personal level to leave us utterly convinced these traditional Original men and women were, for want of a better description (when none exists), a nation of Jesuses and Marys. And if that observation is a little too unsettling, at the very least they could make claim to be a community of Adams and Eves.

The spiritually arid paradigm of scientistic materialism treats death as yet another meaningless experience in the endless progression of meaningless events that have happened since the big bang. Its only solution to the pain of death is to delay it as long as possible—if not indefinitely in the transhumanist fantasy of uploading one's consciousness, presumably so the meaninglessness of existence can be indefinitely prolonged. In contrast to this, from the Original perspective imbued with the spirit of the Dreaming, mortality is a blessing, an opportunity, and a time to rest and reflect after each incarnation. There is no real mystery in the process, just varying degrees of faith the individual applies to the equation. And there were no people that better understood what the circle of life encompasses than the traditional Original women and men of Australia. The oft quoted but rarely understood declaration, "it's a good day to die" is a cliché, an enigma, and the reason why we are deposited on this rotating rock.

In Western society, no day is a good day to die, and many go to inordinate lengths and expense to avoid the inevitable. In traditional Original society, every day is a good day to die, and everyone spent a great deal of time and ceremony embracing the eternal. In days steeped in traditional law and lore, everything, even death, was the lifeblood of a stable lifestyle and society that had been in existence since the Dreaming.

Once one has come to grips with the manifestations of the separation between the perishable and eternal, there are other secrets to be learned. Aware of the circular game and role of karma, knowing why is a solid foundation but still leaves plenty of room for who, what, and when. The days and seconds that make up each incarnation provide both temptations and opportunities. What to do, when, and who are responsible: these decisions are essential elements of the Dreaming and vital components of an esoteric heritage that was exported abroad in ancient times.

But the greatest gift taken abroad, regardless of whether accepted or denied, is eternal. Never part of history, and always standing apart, the mystical teachings and associated talents were essential elements of the cultural landscape of Australia until the British arrived. Despite the extensive damage, this legacy still exists.

However, it is always unwise to either overstate or embark on a crusade. No matter how altruistic and spiritual these societies were, to claim ancient Australia was quite literally heaven on earth is naïve and untrue. War, disputes, lies, and jealousy are all part and parcel of the human condition, but if trying to create a template for a less than perfect species to live by, the Dreaming was and still is the best earthly model available. But even within the continent and islands of Australia, there were varying degrees of perfection and one location and date that marks possibly the most faithful expression of the Dreaming yet seen.

CHAPTER 10

MYSTICS OR MORONS?

Archaeological evidence has demonstrated that 4,000 years ago the material culture and customs of the Tasmanians changed dramatically.[1]

Anyone who has traveled extensively throughout India will no doubt be accustomed to the sight of naked men at religious ceremonies, often in some form of devotional pose, paying homage to their God. These extreme Hindu mystics are tolerated and venerated in a society that is quite conservative in regard to sexual matters and morality. For that matter, we doubt any culture (with one notable exception) would encourage a naked male to stroll down the street past men, women, and children without anybody raising a complaint or lodging a charge. Regardless, Hindu mystics called *sadhus* are permitted to wander in public completely naked. These men devote their entire life to their vision of God, sacrificing all attachments to the material plane, caring not for clothing, money, or personal comfort. Personal hardships mean nothing when dedicating every second of each day to veneration and meditation.

Thousands of kilometers to the south, there existed an entire nation on one island that lived their lives as *sadhus*. This was a place where everyone—close to 8,000 people—eschewed all forms of material comfort, went naked, and lived a lifestyle that was totally reliant upon the land and their Creation Spirits. Despite lacking deeds of ownership and most material possessions, these people managed to flourish under what may appear to be extremely trying conditions.

Noted colonial artist John Glover created a painting titled "Aborigines Dancing at Brighton, Tasmania." His intention was to depict a scene he witnessed that exemplified the Original "mode of enjoying the country."[2] The artist had set himself the demanding task of depicting the atmosphere of unbridled joy and the amazing dexterity displayed in an Original ceremony, noting that "I have seen more enjoyment and mirth [on] such occasions than I ever saw in a Ballroom in England."[3] In 1772, when the first French explorers made contact with Tasmanian mainland Original people, they were highly impressed by their demeanor and customs and found them to be "exceptionally peaceful, joyous, and open people."[4] Upon the explorers' return to France, news of these proud, dignified people spread and had some considerable impact on Jean-Jacques Rosseau's development of the concept of the *noble savage*.

The people of Tasmania, an island that is equivalent in area to Ireland, distinguished themselves not by what they did and owned, but rather by what they chose not to do and possess. At first glance the list of non-achievements and perceived regressions seems to suggest that their Spartan lifestyle would cast doubt on their development and, perhaps, intelligence. So it may appear, but we believe that their culture was not due to ignorance and incompetence, but a statement of unparalleled wisdom that displayed a deep interconnection with the land and the Ancestral Spirits.

The apparent sins of exclusion are extensive and more than a touch deceptive. Among the claimed deprivations are the inability to create fire by any method other than by carrying it; the abandonment of firestick farming; and the absence of every conceivable fire-making tool, boomerangs, woomeras (spear-throwers), barbed wooden spears, clothes, cloaks, blankets, bone tools to weave hide or fabric, hooks, fish nets, any tool requiring hafting and grinded edges on axe heads.

In what could only add to the stark contrast between mainland Australia and Tasmania, the circumcision ceremonies for boys were markedly different, as were burial and marriage ceremonies. The men of Tasmania were unable to swim, and so the list of divergences from what is considered the norm on the Australian mainland continued. The reasons that could explain why this apparently glaring list of substantial deviations, in relation to the culture and technology of traditional Original society occurred, are far less numerous.

There does seem to be a line in the sand, a time when many tools, dietary and lifestyle choices changed. Around 4,000 years ago all nine Tasmanian tribes (each numbering between 600 and 800 people) decided many issues were in need of drastic revision. Before that decision, their lives were no different than those on the mainland. The archaeological "evidence from ice-age sites suggests that, at the time the island was cut off, the Tasmanians' tool-kit was similar to that of those on the mainland."[5] But once dramatic changes to technology and diet were agreed upon, the differences in tool-kits grew with every passing decade.

The inability of any traditional Tasmanian Original to light a fire with either stick or stone seemed to leave these people at a distinct disadvantage. Instead of creating fire, a respected Elder "in each tribe carried a fire stick that was kept perpetually burning."[6] They were the only Original tribes who decided not to use firestick farming as a tool with which to hunt and clean their tribal estate. Even though this abandonment of firestick farming was restrictive and reminiscent of lesser-developed times humans experienced long ago, we believe it was not borne of ignorance, but an enlightened choice to embrace a more austere existence.

To explain what that choice was and when it was made, we need to step back 4,000 years to understand why certain methods of making fire and certain uses of it, along with many other conveniences, were rejected. Around 4,000 years ago, the artifacts and associated deposits found in middens reveal that "a remarkable change took place."[7] That specific time, very close to 4,000 years ago seems a defining moment, a time where choices were made that led to many omissions and very few additions. Bone tools, which were common until that point, "dropped out of use."[8] This is but one of many sacrifices made on behalf of a greater cause. In a midden at Rocky Cape there were 3,196 fish bones found in the stratum dated between 8,000 and 3,800 years. However, in the younger, upper half of the excavation, only one small fish bone was found, and there is a strong probability that it "could have easily been brought inside by a seal or cormorant."[9] At Little Swanport, a midden contains no fish bones at every level before 3,550 years, but between 3,550 and 4,750 years 13 separate remains of leatherjacket were found.

The trend is consistent: many tools, foods, and luxuries were replaced by new pursuits and less labor-intensive technologies. "Canoe-rafts could hold six or seven people,"[10] but there "is no evidence that watercraft were used in Tasmania before about 4,000 years ago."[11] The use of fire was refashioned into something far more complex. The people's needs had not changed, as fire was still essential for cooking meat and conducting ceremonies, but was also accorded a reverence that reinforced a pivotal lesson that originated out of the first throes of creation. The Elders of each of the nine tribes were given the privilege of maintaining the flame, and if the fire was extinguished through carelessness or mishap, they would seek out a neighboring tribe to help rekindle the flame.

They knew that in the Dreaming, when life began, Biamie left behind a special gift for all people of this continent: fire.

Its first incarnation was in the form of a sacred tree, "which is called the Father of All Fires. This was a magic tree. When the rains fell, after Yondi pushed up the sky, lightning flashed down and set it alight . . . and it was burning ever since. But because it was a magic tree it never burned down."[12]

By adopting an austere and reverent approach, the respect and care given to this flame, a gift from the Ancestral Spirits, is constant. They must be ever vigilant, taking care to ensure nothing could allow the flame to go out, while tending to its constant needs. The Elder who was chosen as custodian of the fire earns, by association as well as through his deeds, respect from all who rely upon him.

The rejection of methods of fire creation other than birthing each new fire from the original sacred flame, and reliance upon sharing and goodwill of another tribe to rekindle the flame, created cooperation and inter-tribal harmony and thus reduced the incidence of dispute and battle.

The colonial botanist aboard the Endeavour, Joseph Banks, when first sighting the Tasmanian Originals, made an observation which was far closer to a lost truth than he could realize. He noted that, "of clothes they have not the least part but naked as ever our general father was before his fall."[13] James Cook was somewhat taken aback by a setting reminiscent of the opening pages of Genesis, and his moral sensibilities were challenged by the fact that the "women do not so much as cover their privates."[14] This predilection towards wearing very little is not peculiar to Tasmania, but is common throughout Australia. However, as the night began to set in and the air chilled, many Originals on the mainland nestled into a possum-skinned coat; blankets made from hide, fabric, or bark; wrapped themselves around dingos; rolled on hot coals; or found some way to keep warm.

The people of Tasmania chose to settle less than 1,000 kilometers from the great Antarctic ice sheet. Even at the peak of the last major Ice Age, when massive icebergs were floating up the coast, they persevered. Despite the severe climatic conditions, they were averse to clothing, rugs, or blankets. This is evident because of the absence of any recovered bone tools, in particular bone points used to sew and stitch fur, skin, and rug. As would be expected, the last archaeological remains of this elemental component of the mainland tool-kit were found in Tasmania 4,000 years ago.

Instead of assuming these choices reflect "a technical degeneracy,"[15] there is an alternative explanation.

It is possible, the "fact that the Tasmanian Aborigines had at one time eaten fish, used bone tools to make skin clothing and used fire more extensively—all of which ceased 4,000 years before European settlement—may not mark a technological degeneracy, but rather a renaissance of the influence of the original law in their daily life and behavior."[16]

As evidenced in every midden in Tasmania, fish bones disappear around 4,000 years ago, as do hooks and nets. During the period they fished, thirty-one different species of fish were caught and disposed of within the various middens examined. Once again some have fallen into the error of passing judgment from a considerable distance when trying to assign an explanation that could justify this apparent anomaly. The reasons fish were ignored had nothing to do with regression or poor choice, but were simply due to good choice, preference, and bounty.

There are many descriptions of Original women swimming through schools of fish on their way to collect abalone and shell-fish. Even when offered fish freely by white settlers, it was refused by all Tasmanian Originals, who "did not seem to regard it as human food."[17] The reason most influential in leading to the entire population changing their diet and lifestyle, was simply because there was a better option available. When taking into account geographic and climatic factors, dietary needs, and the most effective use of resources and labor, fishing was a very poor choice and they did well to be rid of it.

Seals, mutton birds, and possums were plentiful throughout the island; of course this abundance declined dramatically once the white settlers arrived. But before the slaughter began, the many large herds of seals were clumsy and easily clubbed to death. The mutton birds nested on many off-shore islands and the women had no trouble swimming to the islands to collect the birds and their eggs. For the more distant islands where the mutton birds nested, the construction of raft-canoes, capable of sailing up to 15 kilometers of open water, occurred around 4,000 years ago to cater for this improvement in diet.

At the same time, on the land, the men would search for trees whose trunks were covered in claw marks and scale the trees with ease for the possums they knew must be hidden above. All of these food sources were far easier to catch than fish and provided for many more hungry mouths, and this provided a compelling enough reason to reject fish as a desirable food source.

The location, severity of the seasons, and bitterly cold winters created a special dietary requirement for any who chose to maintain a hunter/gatherer lifestyle.

"Hunters in high, cold latitudes need foods rich in fat, yielding high energy. Thus, for the Tasmanians, seals and sea-birds were better than shellfish or fish. Indeed 'Had the Tasmanians the services of a consultant nutritionist, they would probably have been advised to give up fishing and concentrate their efforts on more profitable foods. There is evidence in the past 3,000 B.P. archaeological record that this is just what they did."[18]

In addition to the dietary needs these foods catered for, the oil contained within many types of seals, possum, and mutton bird was extremely efficient in helping Original Australians retain their body heat. Completely naked for four seasons, and lacking blankets or rugs, the oil coated over their body was the only accommodation made to the sub-zero temperatures.

Once they had determined what foods were available and most beneficial to their physical needs when coping with severe climates, they modified the selection of implements and techniques utilized, dramatically remodeling their original tool-kit. Skills and technologies they were familiar with, including the construction of hatchets, boomerangs, woomeras (spear throwers), every form of hafting handles onto stone tools, grinding stone edges, making barbed wooden spears, along with many other sophisticated forms of stone and wood technology were deemed unnecessary to their future requirements. Again, it was a pragmatic response to an undeniable reality. They now hunted seal, mutton bird, possum, and small mammals: for this a rough piece of wood would suffice. When every other tool takes time and considerable effort to construct, a thick branch lying on the ground can kill a seal, mutton bird, or possum just as efficiently. Therefore, once fish and larger mammals became a very small part of their diet, there was no longer a need to spend large amounts of time constructing tools and weapons which no longer served a purpose.

The seal's breeding habits became instilled into the yearly cycle of nearly every Tasmanian tribe. Most tribes spent up to four months camped in quite substantial structures while harvesting seals. At West Point, archaeologists have found "seven or eight circular depressions, about 4 metres across and 0.5 metres deep. It seems certain that these were the foundations of dome-shaped huts, which were in use in historic times in Tasmania."[19] The camp was stationed above a beach where a breeding colony of seals returned each year.

While their prey was on solid ground, the men had a role to play, but once the ocean became the hunting ground, they were delegated to the role of a passive spectator: every traditional Tasmanian Original male was unable to swim, dogpaddle, or make any useful contribution past immediately drowning. In opposition to what occurred in mainland Australia, the men were terrified of the open ocean, believing evil spirits would capture and kill any male who set foot in the water. The reality is, death was a very likely result if they joined the women when gathering abalone and shellfish or swimming to the islands for mutton birds. The cold ocean currents flowing from the Antarctic can quickly cause cramping and hypothermia, and as women possess a much larger amount of subcutaneous fat, they have a greater tolerance to cold water. Acknowledging the prevailing conditions and common sense, only women were permitted to swim in waters so cold.

On many levels Tasmania remains an enigma among Australian Original societies. Many commentators misconstrue the change to a more austere lifestyle is a sign of decline, when it may be the opposite. Yet the mystery of the Tasmanians does not end with their technological progress. Many anthropologists were astounded by the dark skin and thick curly hair of these people, who seemed to share all the physical attributes to those living in equatorial climes. It is undeniable they had far darker skin than any tribe in Victoria or New South Wales, and up until the science of genetics proved all Aborigines shared the same genetic base, many believed that the Tasmanian Originals were a distinct race unrelated to those on the mainland.

Respected anthropologist Norman Tindale considered the differences so stark that there had to be a logical reason for this divergence. His proposed solution was unsustainable and a touch perplexing, but not to be condemned, as his solution was in accord with the facts known at the time.

He suggested there was "a third group of Aborigines whom they called 'Barrineans,' a people living in the north-eastern rain forest from Cairns. They were smaller than other mainland Aborigines, and possibly related to the Tasmanians. The Barrineans could have been a surviving mainland group of the original Tasmanoids who had come to Australia."[20]

Although separated by 30 degrees of latitude, Tindale believed the two tribes were identical in many respects. However, for reasons we find difficult to locate, Tindale paid little attention to the fact that within the entire Barrinean nation of Far North Queensland, rarely, if ever, did either man or woman stand taller than four foot.

Genetics has since discounted this explanation through division, but no further explanation has been proposed to explain how people living in climatic conditions similar to that experienced by Eskimos retained the skin color and physique of those living in the tropics. In every equivalent geographic region, whether it be Siberia, Patagonia, or Sweden, the indigenous people are fair-skinned, thin-lipped, and have fine hair. Then there is Tasmania, the same distance from the equator, but with one difference: the people of that country were dark-skinned, thick-lipped, and had thick, curly hair.

The differences between the Tasmanian Originals and every other Original tribe were not just restricted to physique, technology, diet, and art, but extended into many aspects of their religious life. "They were an uncircumcised race,"[21] which in itself has no mainland parallel, but the elemental differences in what may appear as social and religious constants do reinforce the notion these people made a conscious decision in deciding that nearly all of what was occurring in the rest of Australia was unworthy of emulation. Many other facets of mainland religious life were either discarded or amended to suit their more rigorous requirements, and as a result, they also had "markedly different marital and burial traditions"[22] from all mainland tribes.

If the Tasmanian Original people were as primitive and technologically backward as many propose, why was it that their resistance so concerned the white invaders that the government passed an edict insisting that genocide was the only effective means of countering the threat they posed? The level of resistance, effectiveness of their tactics, and skilled bushcraft made them formidable adversaries. Strategies used by Europeans in other parts of the colony were useless in this terrain and against their intelligence and skill. It appears they quickly adapted to the changing conditions of its inhabitants. When driven off the plains and into the mountains, they built many stone huts and stored food stolen from the settlers. These sites became bases from which to launch their guerrilla warfare. All of this occurred without the benefit of fishing, cloaks, firesticks, or sophisticated stone tools, but with the wisdom of the ages sourced directly from the Dreaming.

"As early as 1830 there was a 'tradition of implacable hostility' toward the white man. Original resistance was very effective. At least 200 white men were killed and observers were impressed by Original tactics and generalship. In 1828 the colony's Executive Council advised the Governor that terrorism was the only effectual security for the colonists. Originals were banned from all settlements, martial law was declared, and rewards were offered for their capture—5 pounds for adults and 2 pounds for children."[23]

For a supposedly stagnated, ignorant people to be able to cause so much consternation, verging on impotence, beggars belief. That the British military should resort to outright genocide in countering the danger posed by these naked women and men brandishing sticks and stones reflects how ineffective they were in fighting the Original Tasmanians. To sell their soul and morality for between two and five pounds a body, regardless of guilt or age, reflects a desperation and complete lack of ethics which inevitably led to the annihilation of the Tasmanian mainland nation of the nine confederated tribes.

In 1830 Tasmanian Governor Arthur decided to take the initiative, as all other efforts had failed, and to put it bluntly, if the soldiers weren't losing, they certainly were not wining. Arthur convened the infamous *Black Line*, at an eventual cost of over 35,000 pounds, beginning with an assemblage of over 5,000 settlers and soldiers at Hobart. Their brief was simple: to capture, but preferably kill, any person of dark complexion they came upon as they scoured southeastern Tasmania. Whether innocent or a child still unable to walk, all were to be treated equally and captured, or more than likely dispatched, without mercy. Six weeks of earnest endeavor clambering through extremely steep terrain saw a scorecard where the first round was won narrowly by the native Tasmanians. "Two Aboriginals were shot and two captured. Five white men were killed in accidents."[24]

It became obvious that the combined stealth and skill of the militia was to no avail when battling against such a cunning and intelligent foe. The whites had to rely upon the one talent they excelled in—deception and outrageous lies. In this pernicious area their arsenal was massive, cleverly camouflaged, and gave the Tasmanian Original people little in the way of defense. The invaders' secret weapon was not recognized or expected. The traditional Original people had no understanding or word to express the concept of lying. Once this weapon was loaded, all that was needed was a sheep in wolves' clothing to deliver their duplicitous message.

Governor Arthur appointed Reverend George Augustus Robinson to the position of Protector of the Aborigines. His duty was simple: to deceive the Originals with descriptions of a mythical paradise, replete with native animals, bush tucker (food found in the Australian Outback), trees, and peace. Of course there was a cost, to gain admission to the place Robinson described as the "Great Island," the immediate cessation of all conflict with settlers and soldiers had to occur. After months of traveling the countryside, Robinson convinced all of the Originals his word was his bond. Unarmed and vowing to speak the truth with his God's blessing and book, his promises exuded sincerity and his smile was so full of warmth. Trusting in this man, the Originals laid down their weapons and followed him to discover that the Promised Land was far less idyllic than promised.

The forests, streams, and bountiful bush tucker of the fabled "Great Island" gave way to the overwhelming reality of Flinders Island. When first sighting their new prison, some "moaned and shook"[25] with despair. The barren treeless outpost, lacking in fertile land or any source of bush tucker, was too much to bear. Once marooned on this concentration camp where the sea replaced barbed wire, the last survivors gave up all hope. All that they could do was sit and stare out into the ocean and the distant shoreline of Tasmania, while waiting to die. Barely ten years after incarceration of the remaining mainland Originals of Tasmania, 156 of the 200 exiles were dead, and twenty years past that point, Truganini (the last mainland Tasmanian Original woman) died.

They were the last survivors of a people that made a decision to adopt a lifestyle where the "material culture is the simplest known anywhere in the world."[26]

As a result, these sacrifices carried over into every aspect of their culture, and necessitated that when expressing themselves artistically, they used motifs and symbols that "reflect the oldest cultural patterns."[27]

When tracking the development of the variety of artistic traditions scattered throughout Australia, it is widely accepted that the most ancient is the Panaramitee Tradition. It is an amalgam of geometric shapes and lines and is thought to have first begun at either Panaramitee (>75,000 years, Lake Eyre, S.A.), Jinmium (<115,000 years, Keep River, NT), or the more controversial option of Devonport (>115,000 years, Tasmania).

The eight accepted engraving sites in Tasmania all remain faithful to the Panaramitee Tradition, but are a very recent addition and claimed by the academics to be created in the last 4,000 years. This style of rock engraving is the only type of artistic expression used throughout the island. With the exception of one set of bird tracks at Mount Cameron, all of the thousand-odd engravings found in Tasmania strictly adhere to the ancient stylized patterns present at Panaramitee and Jinmium.

The style of engraving at "Mount Cameron West and other sites in Tasmania . . . show all the same qualitative features as Panaramitee engravings—enough to say they are essentially in the same style . . . the range of motifs, their technique, their form, and their size are identical."[28] The salient point being "the Panaramitee Tradition is Australia's oldest artistic system and seems to have a continent-wide distribution."[29]

Cameron West (Mount Cameron) is the most prolific and extensively studied site in Tasmania containing 404 circular engravings. Apart from circles, which make up 45% of all icons found, there are many dots and lines. Putting aside the cultural and historical significance of this site, the aesthetic values of the artwork are worthy of admiration, as it "is widely recognized as the oldest and most outstanding artistic achievement of any hunter-gatherer society."[30]

All eight sites in Tasmania share the same symbols, and are claimed to be of relatively recent construction, but there are other places that are far more ancient and were not subject to the more recent trend of engraving. At a time well before the first cave wall in Tasmania was thought to have been engraved, the Originals painted with ochre.

The antiquity of Tasmanian art is still in dispute, but an agreed base age of 34,790 B.P. is accepted. Five ochred hand stencils were found on a cave wall. Hand stencils have been found elsewhere, but as yet this is the oldest documented date. With the exception of hand stencils, no other cave walls in Tasmania reveal any other style of art involving ochre. Once this form of stenciling was abandoned, it would appear for a substantial period of time nothing was apparently created. After over 20,000 years of artistic abstinence their local inhabitants' creative energies re-emerge to be chaneled into one agreed style of engraving on rock walls.

Again, this course of action, or perhaps inaction is a more appropriate term, has no precedent in any corner of the globe. If the Original people were using ochre 35,000 years ago to create the outline of their hands, why didn't this basic technique evolve as it did elsewhere? Mainland Original people were using ochre, blood, saliva, vegetable dye, animal fat, charcoal, beeswax, and any other local material that was available to express their creativity and satisfy their religious obligations. The elaborate X-Ray art of Arnhem Land painted on cave walls, the intricate Gwoin Gwoin (Bradshaw) figures, and enigmatic Wandjinas of the Kimberely region were painted in sacred locations and are fine pieces of art, irrespective of time, culture, or associated meanings. The Papunya art tradition is a blend of symbols and lines

painted on a background of dots and imbued with layers of mystical meaning. Contemporary paintings created with that style as its
prime inspiration, have sold for millions of dollars. But in Tasmania,
the pinnacle of their artistic endeavors was to spit colored mud and
saliva onto their hand and the surrounding rock wall and then call it
a day.

Every other Original Australian culture's artistic tradition begins
with a few dabs of color and a simple design or figure and then
expands upon the use of this medium to develop a unique region-
specific style and content. Australia, the place where art originated,
is the best available example of how incredibly diverse this creative
process became. However, Tasmanians appears to contradict this
mainland trend. Instead they decided to discard ochre and do nothing for millennia upon millennia. Then finally the urge to express
oneself artistically seems to reappear, whereby the whole population
of the island chooses one medium, one technique, and one tradition.
Engraving into rock in the Panaramitee Tradition was acceptable;
nothing else was appropriate or created past that point.

All eight engraving sites exhibit the same techniques and
subject matter. Once again this is unique: nowhere on the mainland do nine adjoining tribes share identical styles and symbols.
A multitude of distinct artistic styles and all manner of depictions
co-exist yet remain within strictly delineated tribal boundaries. On
the mainland, each tribe had their own Creation Spirit, with associated stories, geographic formations, and events that were created for
their specific tribal estate. In Tasmania, the nine mainland tribes tolerated no bickering or deviations from agreed standards and shared
common dietary, technological, and artistic traditions as one homogenous group.

Of course, when naming the tradition of rock engravings found
throughout Tasmania, the academics have referred to the site from
which they claimed the style originated. Their proclamation was not
based on a Dreaming story, oral tradition, or Original Australian artifacts, but on a date obtained by the most recent advances in science

and technology. Others, who rely on less sophisticated procedures and inspiration, are less convinced the laboratory can supply the answer to these questions. One Elder claims that neither Panaramitee nor Jinmium was the first site where this artistic tradition began, but it was the Tasmanian Original people who first created the tradition of engraving these shapes into rock, and was subsequently shared with their sisters and brothers to the north (this would have occurred well before the separation of the land bridge at around 8,000 years).

Tinker Gowan, a Devonport Elder and custodian of sacred sites, strongly disagrees that this is a recent addition and has no doubt that the rock engravings spread around the headland at Devonport are much, much older and predate the engravings at Jinmium. He claims the style and selection of icons were decided upon in Tasmania, at a time when the island was attached to the mainland. Once established, the techniques and symbols have remained unaltered, regardless of the appearance of the many styles and trends occurring in other places. The nine tribes steadfastly adhered to the original tradition.

On the opening page of respected archaeologist Josephine Flood's book, *Rock Art of the Dreamtime,* she began her chapter by sharing details of a book launch and a question she was constantly asked in relation to Tasmanian culture: "Why didn't they progress and become civilized?"[31]

As stated earlier, many academics have adopted the same superficial approach when assessing the attainments of the Tasmanian Original people. The judgments passed by the experts reek of an ingrained ethnocentric bias that can be traced back to the first time there was conflict between hunter-gatherer societies and those who farmed the land and claimed ownership. In what can only compound the affront, these people were considered unable to rub two sticks together and start a fire. Those who equate progress with restless change, technology, and books were unsettled by many aspects of the Spartan material culture of the Tasmanian Originals. What they never saw was that this supposed regression was not a result of ignorance, but solely the product of an enlightened choice. At a certain point in their history, these people reverted back to the original ways, using only what was really needed and staying as close as they could to the rhythm and needs of the land.

Some who are sympathetic to the Original cause and culture have tried to defend these supposed inadequacies, but are blinded by a perspective couched in materialism. Instead of recognizing the Tasmanians' ascetic Spartan practices as pathways that enable closer contact with the land and their Creator, cultural biases have clouded many judgments. Despite her good intentions, Josephine Flood's attempted defense of the Original Tasmanians fails to identify the virtue in their choice.

"Another myth that should be laid to rest is that Tasmanian Aborigines did not know how to make fire. The only evidence for this is that Robinson never observed anyone making fire because fire-sticks were always carried. An argument based on flimsy negative evidence is always suspect, and it seems unlikely that the Tasmanians could have made some of the water crossings that they did, such as those to Hunter, King and Maatsuyker Islands, and kept fires alight on hearths in the boats during the whole voyage."[32]

Middens over the past 4,000 years bear witness to a dramatic decrease in charcoal deposits, and no traditional Original or set-tler ever claimed to have observed the process occurring. There is no fire-making artifact found to substantiate Flood's claim in any midden studied, and no historical account of any Tasmanian Original making fire. To put it simply, it is a "defense" without a shred of evidence. The reality is that the lack of fire-making is not in need of defending as it does not indicate a deficiency. The decision to banish the art of fire-making was not the outcome of some form of cultural stagnation, but represented an enlightened choice of lifestyle and an act of homage through simplification.

The title of this chapter was intended to reflect a truth in oppo-sition to an unspoken supposition that betrays the prejudice and pre-conditioning of the dominant society. Many use a system of values based on greed and the idolatry of the material world as measuring sticks to determine how much a culture has attained. In spite of this popular malpractice, there is a more logical and noble standard of measure.

It may have been that "the fact that the Tasmanian Aborigines had at one time eaten fish, used bone tools to make skin clothing, and used fire more extensively—may not mark a technological degeneracy, but rather a renaissance of the influence of the original law in their daily life and behavior."[33]

The reality is, the rejection of so many conveniences, from blankets to making fire, was either the choice of mystics or morons. We have no doubt that within a region which was the source for all myths extolling the Garden of Eden, there was one island lived a people who were the most fervently committed to staying in contact with the spirits of the land. The choices made by the Original Tasmanian nation of mystics, who chose to live the life of *sadhus*, confused many and incurred the disdain of white settlers. This confusion was only accentuated by their very existence and eventual annihilation. Their pigmentation, hair, lips, along with their choice to forgo the fruits of the bone needle, run counter to their location and Darwinism. Unlike the Inuit, Lapp, Siberian, or any other straight-haired, narrow-nosed inhabitant from like latitudes, the physical features of the Tasmanian are contrary to theory and unlike their neighbors. They are claimed by Tindale to resemble Original Australians near Cairns, and by Robert Lawlor to share identical semantic traits to the Dravidians of Southern India. In both cases, the comparisons are made to people from tropical climes.

The stance of these people, in choosing to sacrifice many conveniences that make life a little more comfortable and predictable, raises a fundamental issue as to what constitutes progress. Will our welfare and well-being be dependent upon more white goods, bigger plasma screens, and smarter computers? Every day a scientist or company develops a new commodity that is reputed to make someone's life easier. Whatever the blessing endowed upon the purchaser, it will always be transitory, as the newer and more expensive version will soon be on the shelves. And so the cycle repeats and spreads until it no longer becomes a means to an end, but becomes both means and end.

The traditional Original Tasmanians knew that coveting material objects led to addiction and division. The changes to their technology and lifestyle were essential if they were to remove any temptation or obstacle that would impede the soul's progress. By spurning any device or lifestyle that widened the gap between the soul and the Dreaming, they believed they would become more spiritual and less attached to earthly desires and distractions.

Of one point we are convinced, the perceived impoverished state of affairs in Tasmania was achieved through design and not the result of degeneration. The chances of it being otherwise are as great as it turning out that the Amish prefer the horse and cart to the car because they are intellectually unable to adapt to the new technology.

As to whether the Tasmanians' interpretation of the Dreaming is at its most pristine is a subjective call, but if any comparison was to be made, we must remain within Australia. Elsewhere, beyond the reach of the continental shelf, the shadows and additions have diluted the essence of what the Dreaming prescribed, but within this country there are many other tribes worthy of comparison. Whether they, too, match the intensity and devotion of the nine tribes from the Tasmanian mainland is a question that can never have a definitive answer.

To do justice to the legacy of the Original Australians is to accept that there is an underlying inspiration underpinning all religions, that has a supreme intrinsic spiritual value rather than merely being of interest to theologians and scholars of comparative religion. Yet given the contemporary values that reign unchallenged in much of the world, this all amounts to very little in pragmatic terms. By this measure their sole contribution was to the paradigms of superstition and illusion. They were naked, nomadic, and deliberately eschewing all technology not based in sticks, stones, and bones. Both critic and commentator could justifiably ask, of what benefit to the global community were these ancient voyages?

This question and the mistaken assumptions that now permeate book and curriculum, weigh heavily upon the heart, soul, and dignity of Australian Originals past and present, and illustrate once again how much of their past was lost, forgotten, or ignored. Nor is it justified, even if we consider technological development alone. The Original people of the mainland were far more sophisticated than has generally been acknowledged, and may well have been the originators of much of the knowledge that formed the beginnings of human technology, worldwide, as we shall see in our next chapter.

CHAPTER 11

THE SHIP'S CARGO

Encyclopedias, academic texts, and experts all echo the same tune, dismissing the Ancient Australians as technological minnows. An authoritative commentary which was distributed to every Australian school in the 1960s somewhat typically alleged, "the Australian Aborigine shares ... the distinction of being the most primitive race of man,"[1] and that "the aborigine [sic] lagged behind in the march of progress, and so lingered in the Old Stone Age."[2] If this is so, then one could rightly declare that, even if they did set sail 50,000 years ago, their journey would have brought no benefits to humanity. Were they, indeed, so far at the rear of the "march of progress,"[3] ignorant of the advantages of money and modernity, incapable of crafting a bow, arrow, or wheel, whether they did or didn't sail seems irrelevant.

Perhaps, but history is often a victor's valedictory speech where the vanquished are ignored or slandered. Unfortunately, this is very much the case with the white version of Original Australian history. So little was seen or accurately reported. The absence of the bow and arrow in the Original Australian technological tool-kit is considered damning evidence of the race's inferiority. This would be offensive enough if it were true; however, an entry in Captain James Cook's journal made on August 22, 1770, reveals that this particular pillar, used to shore up the invader's chauvinism, is as rotten as the rest. Cook reported that, after setting anchor, he and his crew were surprised to see "one man who had a bow and bundle of arrows, the first we had seen on this coast."[4] The people Cook saw were living, in every conceivable sense, a communal and egalitarian lifestyle where personal acquisition and monopolies were unknown. If one person was carrying a bow and arrows, then many more knew what it was and how it was made. Therefore, the bow and arrow was common knowledge and in existence before Cook sailed up the east coast of Australia. As to whether these weapons were carried aboard in distant times when sailing to foreign locations can never be proven, but of one reality there is no doubt. When archaeologists and historians debate over when and where the bow and arrow was invented, Australia is neither a rumor nor candidate.

What the Ancient Original people took with them when they sailed from Australia to distant lands can only be speculated upon. Undeniably, the longer the gap in time, the greater the uncertainties involved when determining what occurred. In most places the "march of progress" is an eccentric form of locomotion, which often proceeds through warfare and commerce as society develops and spreads. But in Australia, until the British invasion, there was a continental decision to embrace a frugal hunter-gatherer lifestyle and live in balance with nature. Once an implement/technique was found to be effective, there was no need to reinvent the tool. As such, Australian technology shows little variation and has an extremely long "shelf life." Just as with the spiritual outlook of the people, it being totally adequate to its purpose, the idea of improvement or "progress" is ludicrous.

It is true that the technological resources of the Ancient Australians were limited when compared to that of other cultures and times. Yet, it could also be maintained that there was very little that is essential to a good life which was missing. Certainly it is true that, limited as it was, it was vastly more extensive than is generally known and contains some extremely sophisticated techniques and items of knowledge. These reveal the inadequacy of the conception of the Original Australians' modest collection of technological accoutrements as being due to "primitivism."

As it stands the current assumption is akin to maintaining that anyone who doesn't walk around balancing 50 kilos of steel weights on their head is lacking in the coordination, stamina, and intelligence required to do so. While this might be the case, one might be forgiven for thinking that it is more likely due to the fact that most people lack the strange frame of mind that would make such a thing seem desirable in the first place. The difference in the two positions is the difference between those who see "progress" as easing the white man's burden and those who see it as a millstone around his neck.

Nor are we blind to those accomplishments of human understanding and technological skill that do improve life and give us some advantages over other species who must survive without them. It is precisely these that the Ancient Australians did have and that may well have originated here. There are many devices and branches of knowledge that were known here long ago and were very likely exported abroad, among which we would include brain surgery, amputation, dentistry, penicillin, the axe, art, burial, singing to dolphins, running/walking on the water, navigation by the stars. All of this as well as the philosophy of the Dreaming.

In the rest of this chapter we will look more closely at the evidence of the antiquity of the presence of this knowledge in Australia.

THE FIRST CUT

According to Dr. Denise Conlan, an Original skull dated to be over 400 years old which she examined was, without doubt, evidence of "an early form of brain surgery. Bone growth showed the patient survived."[5] Professor Noel Dann was taken aback by the obvious sophistication of the Original surgeon as "the trepidation (cutting) had been performed skilfully, so as to minimise bleeding."[6] The pressing need to publicize this startling find was not lost on the professor. He was aware the hole in the skull defied the expectations of his colleagues and was compelled to declare that "I regard it as absolutely mind-blowing, a great tribute to Aboriginal skills ... it could change the public perception of Aboriginal culture."[7] It could have, but Dann's hopes soon spiraled into the same academic void as did a similar announcement made nearly fifty years earlier.

First recovered by respected archaeologist Isabel McBryde at Blaxland's Flat (*Bundjalung* Language Confederation), a skull, which she named "individual 4,"[8] (dated as 1,250 years old) has a "hole"[9] measuring 4.4cms × 2.4cms. What was decidedly unusual was the nature of the "hole,"[10] which bore "a clean ... bevelled edge"[11] with "no cracking or splitting of the inner or outer tables in the area this opening."[12] McBryde was of the opinion the hole was made before death ("premortem"[13]) and was not "the result of a hard blow on the skull."[14] She also discounted the impact of disease, simply because "disease conditions which produce such holes in the skull were not, as far as we know, present in Australia prior to white settlement."[15] That being the case, McBryde was forced to state the obvious: "Although trephination has not been recorded amongst the Australian Aborigines this hole is strongly reminiscent of the practice."[16]

McBryde was uncomfortable with what she had found, hence her equivocation, and sought out the assistance of more sophisticated technology and the advice of colleague Alan Thorne to determine the validity of what the find suggested. Thorne's corroboration of her finding, in which he noted that "the hole is strongly reminiscent of the practice"[17] of brain surgery, gave McBryde the necessary support to publish her paper. Thorne was no less puzzled by the precision and lack of fraying. "The specimen displays a curious oval-shaped hole (44mm × 26mm) lying longitudinally on the left parietal 35mm from the sagittal suture and just crossing the coronal suture. There is no cracking or fragmentation of either the inner or outer tables in the area around the opening."[18]

Despite the standing of the academics who were both prepared to consider the real possibility that "individual 4"[19] survived brain surgery, this paper, and that on the recent examination of the 400-year-old skull, barely caused a ripple in the sea of indifference and presupposition. Of course, these dates barely span a millennium and, until we are dealing with five figures, any claims regarding what cargo and insights were present among Australia's first exports can only be tenuous possibilities.

Found in the solidified mud at Lake Mungo, and dated at somewhere between 19,000 and 23,000 years, "one curious set of footprints appears to have been made by a one-legged man."[20] That an Original amputee was walking in the mud 20,000 years ago is an unsupportable interpretation if we rely on conventional historical paradigms.

So long as we uphold this bias, it seems reasonable to assert that, "it is unlikely that someone would have survived an amputation in this hunter-gatherer society,"[21] and some explanations for this anomalous find have to be concocted.

The two suggestions offered to explain away this enigmatic set of prints are as contradictory as they are unsubstantiated. Aware the footprints do indeed form a steady "one-legged"[22] trail, "some archaeologists suggest he was playing a hopping game with a child, whose smaller footprints appear alongside. Others think he may have had one leg in a boat, propelling himself along with the other through shallow water."[23]

To begin with, if the adult was hopping, the whole foot would be planted in the ground, if he was pushing forward whilst kneeling in a boat, the heel print wouldn't be visible and the toes would be wedged forward with the weight displacement being dramatically different; either way both options can't be right at the same time. What is even more "unlikely"[24] was the one-legged propulsion of the boat, especially since the "child, whose smaller footprints appear alongside,"[25] was not allowed to sit in the boat with the adult. Without being experts in geology, it also seems unlikely to us that footprints pressed into mud submerged under water would make the same print as those exposed to air and sun.

Alternatively, while it may be possible for an adult to indulge in a "hopping game,"[26] it is equally possible that a people who were capable of successfully performing complex brain surgery before any European set foot in Australia would have no trouble suturing a wound and stemming the flow of blood while amputating a limb. Apparently the child did not join in the game initiated by the adult, so why continue hopping if shunned by an unappreciative audience? Perhaps it was an overgrown child being led by a dwarf?

It is a pity that so much imagination is expended on working out why these prints only appeared to be evidence of amputation rather than on why it might have been actual evidence. There have been a variety of obsidian blades found throughout the country, and the edges are sharp and hard enough to cut bone; past that point all that is needed is the knowledge of how and where to cut. If amputation did occur over 20,000 years ago, the chances are much greater that this surgical technology and knowledge were available when the first explorers departed from Australia, but a large gap in time, although diminishing, still remains. However, when examining what happened to WLH3, who is dated between 45,000 and 65,000 years, the shortfall no longer exists.

THE FIRST DENTIST

It must be granted that the age estimate of this case provided by Alan Thorne based on three different forms of analysis has many opponents, principally Jim Bowler. He dismisses Thorne's radical calculations (61–65,000 years) preferring the more conservative date of 45,000 years. But in what does seem a paradox, he co-wrote a paper with Gurdup Singh and Peter Ouwendyke in 1983, proposing that they had discovered evidence of Original Australian occupation in core samples extracted from the Great Barrier Reef, through the sudden appearance of firestick farming 180,000 years ago. Nevertheless, either date sits comfortably with the notion of Ancient Australian sailors leaving these shores some 50,000 years ago. On this occasion what was found inside the grave occupied by WLH3 is now contemporary with our proposed date of departure and highly likely to be part of whatever was shared with people from other lands.

If any person was to allow someone to pull out their two front teeth, issues relating to bleeding, infection, pain, and a convincing reason to endure this ordeal would need to be addressed before volunteering to take a seat in any dentist's chair. It is a complicated medical procedure, and of extreme importance that "WLH3 had also lost his two lower canine teeth simultaneously when he was much younger."[27] Knowing this must have occurred outside in the open, the chances of infection and complications are increased and demand a strict observance of hygiene and techniques to stem the flow of blood. Tooth avulsion was used in this region as a form of initiation, and is also evidenced with WLH22. Such were the obvious ceremonial implications associated with this painful ritual, Josephine Flood made note that, "if these are actually cases of tooth avulsion . . . this is the oldest instance of the practice anywhere in the world."[28] If so, with this being "the oldest instance"[29] of tooth avulsion, it is not unreasonable to assume this ceremony was originally an Original ritual. Not only was this extraction inspired by mystical concerns, according to Flood, "it would also be further evidence for the great antiquity of Aboriginal religious beliefs."[30]

But it doesn't stop at some bizarre dental work: the religious inspiration behind this procedure is evident from the liberal scattering of red ochre, the pigment most sacred to the Original Australians, around and on the corpse. When coupled with the positioning of the skeleton, with both hands holding his penis, which was exactly how the local Original people of that region disposed of their dead until the British invasion, it seems highly likely that these two conventions were of spiritual significance.

With the first indications of a religious sensibility occurring at Lake Mungo, and at least one related ceremony, tooth avulsion, taking place in Australia tens of thousands of years before anywhere else, an indication of the rites of passage included in the spiritual cargo in this boat begin to take form. Steven Webb is confident this male was subject to the wear and tear of constant spear-throwing; he feels the severe case of osteoarthritis is "suggestive of spear-thrower's elbow."[31] With the crew ready, spear aboard, religious perspective present, dental skills apparent, and the possibility of bows and arrows resting on the ship's deck, there is still room for more.

"THERE SHOULD NOT BE ANY DISEASES."[32]

Penicillin is considered one of the wonder drugs of the twentieth century, but arguments still continue in relation to the input of the two main researchers: the Englishman Alexander Fleming and

Australian Howard Florey. As to what role Florey played is of no interest in general to us. What is of relevance is the acknowledged influence traditional Original Elders had in directing Florey to the curative powers of a certain type of fungus. He was alerted to a species that grew on the shady side of one tree; its properties and effects are identical to penicillin.

This great medicinal advance of the twentieth century was already known when Cook illegally raised the Union Jack, and was an integral part of all Original societies which, given their highly conserved nature, could well have stretched back as far as the rest of the culture. It is extensively reported, often in the most condescending terms, that traditional Original people believed that in their prime years they could not become sick via the agency of germ or virus. If an adult was stricken by some form of suffering, this could only be due to sorcery or offending the spirits.

However, Original people did recognize that those in their formative and declining years could fall prey to an occasional illness and because of this developed an extensive knowledge of natural herbs, medicines, poultices, and the like.

Michael Ryan was raised by an Original Australian nanny/wet nurse during the nineteenth century and accepted as part of the tribe. His description of the roles and powers of the *Wireenen* bears witness to the effectiveness of the native physician even if he lacked degrees and access to the European pharmacopeia.

"The Doctor, also called *Wireenen,* is a specialist. He has reached a greater degree of learning than an Elder. He has had special instruction from other Doctors, and has gone through a special ceremony to fit him for the position. He is not a charlatan; he does not use his position in his tribe for gain as we know it… He is not a doctor in the sense that he cures diseases, because there should not be any diseases. His laws were made to breed people who did not get any disease. He has no word for disease, so he calls any ailment a *Wunda*—a Devil"[33] …"The Aboriginal was the cleanest man on earth. He had no disease of any kind to give the white man. He did not have to cure disease because he did not have any."[34]

THE FIRST BOAT

With the health and welfare of the crew catered for, there are some pragmatic considerations and tools of the trade that were not only exported abroad, but essential to the journey and actual making of the boat. Mentioned previously are a variety of paintings scattered throughout the Kimberleys depicting designs of ocean-going boats that could be as old as 50,000 years. The oldest axe in the world comes from ancient Australia, whether it be the one found at Huon Terrace, PNG (40,000 years) or Jaowyn land, NT (35,500 years). This implement is an essential one for anyone intending to build a boat which could accommodate over twenty people.

Bull-roarers, an iconic Australian religious device used to announce men's business, have been found throughout the world. German anthropologist Hermann Klaatsch's collection of bull-roarers gathered in his field trips throughout the world all share the same esoteric purpose. He was of the opinion the original prototype was made in Australia.

In ancient Greece, as it was and still is in Australia, the bull-roarer was considered a sacred object which could facilitate direct contact with the spirits. An account by the ancient Greek scholar Aeschylus graphically depicts the mystical effect of this instrument. "And bull-voices roar hereto from somewhere out of the unseen, fearful semblances, and from an image as it were of thunder underground is borne on the air with heavy dread."[35] The ancient Greeks claimed it to be "the voice of Supernatural Beings."[36] Mircea Eliade was also aware of the consistency in function and of its pre-Hellenistic inspiration, noting that descriptions of its form and intent are "strangely reminiscent of the Australian and Siberian" accounts.[37]

Of course, the Original men and women who set sail must have been conversant with the sea and its resources, and would have shared knowledge of nets, sail-making, and sundry tools needed to harvest the sea's bounty, but it is worth remembering these people only made tools and devices as a last resort. It was always a matter of what they carried in their hearts and heads that was most vital, and not what they held in their hands.

Consider this photograph which is most definitely not, as described, "a large group of tribesmen spearing fish in the Coomera River."[38] None of the twenty-three warriors carries a spear. Granted one man is holding a leafy branch which may well startle an unsuspecting fish, but there isn't one weapon visible, nor should there be.

They were not "spearing fish,"[39]—the photograph, unlike the commentary, doesn't lie—but they were catching fish. This phenomenon is the subject of many Dreaming stories and magistrates' reports, and we have been privileged to hear personal accounts of it. These men were fishing with their aquatic brothers and sisters, the dolphins. The branch flayed against the water, accompanied by the Elder (standing with hands outstretched) singing a sacred song, is ample incentive for a tribe of dolphins to hunt with these men. The Original fishermen stood in the shallow water and waited for the fish to be driven towards them. The catch was always divided evenly between the two tribes, and this fishing practice was a common one throughout the lands of the *Bundjalung* confederation.

As to whether this mode of cooperative resource management was in existence 50,000 years ago can never be proven in absolute terms, but what can be declared with complete conviction was that this congress between species was at least still occurring in the 1990s. I have spoken to an Original male present at an event he will never forget, and there is no way a man of his integrity would lie about such important traditional business. This man, Brian, along with many of his friends and family, was taken aback by what two Elders loaded into their small dinghy, or rather, what they didn't take: no bait, tackle, hook, or line was visible. Their tactics were as ancient as they were a part of Original lore. What took place was not an attempt to feed the masses or satisfy the hunger; it was a statement of mystical power and a lesson in the "old ways." Catching and cooking fish were minor considerations. These two Elders were seated in the dinghy in the river at least two kilometers from the sea, and when they began to sing in lingo, none seated on the banks understood or recognized the song. Somewhere offshore, a pod of dolphins responded to the call, as had their ancestors many years earlier.

Brian claimed he was the first to sight the approaching dorsal fins. Soon after, the river exploded, fish were fleeing from the line of dolphins, and many saw only one avenue of escape. Such was the quantity and weight of incoming fish now writhing in the boat, there was a real chance it would capsize under the load. With extreme care, assisted by the jettisoning of quite a few fish, they managed to reach the bank. Honoring traditional protocol, the dolphins were fed first, the humans had to wait their turn.

No, this is not a scene from *Doctor Doolittle*, but an example of how powerful secret business is and a further elucidation of the possibilities of what could have been exported aboard. The next aquatic skill that may qualify as possible cargo challenges the laws of physics and will unsettle many cynics. According to the Bible, Jesus walked on water. However, according to two ship's captains and one of the world's most respected nineteenth century anthropologists—Dr. Hermann Klaatsch—Original Australian men and women could not only walk, but run on water. Unlike the Biblical account, which has no independent corroboration, this activity was witnessed not once, but on three separate occasions over an eighty-year period. Both the captains, who came before Klaatsch and were greeted with these displays of phenomenal athleticism, were highly regarded and were working for the Government, delivering them provisions. Part of their brief was to carefully report on all contact with the Original people.

This phenomenon was first reported by Captain Breamer in 1824 when setting anchor just off a beach at Melville Island. He was totally unprepared for the greeting ceremony. His description, if anything, is an understatement of staggering dimensions. Breamer was circumspect when giving specifics but did concede the people there possessed "wonderful elasticity . . . their activity was astonishing."[40] Hermann Klaatsch (1905) was fully prepared for their welcome, observing that "the manner in which they came to my boat reminded me absolutely of the picture published by Captain King, vol 1, p.112."[41] Forewarned by journal entries and King's photograph, Klaatsch was still quite shocked by this communal feat of seemingly miraculous proportions. They "sprang into the water and made towards the boat with surprising celerity, jumping at each step entirely out of the sea, although it was so deep as to reach their thighs."[42]

It is possible when Original Australians set sail from their homeland, they took with them axes, bull-roarers, spears, bows and arrows, obsidian blades to operate with, penicillin, and paint. Furthermore, these people were familiar with religion, complex surgical procedures, a rudimentary form of dentistry, and blessed with perfect health and the ability to talk to dolphins and "run on water." As to whether this wisdom was known 50,000 years ago or 500 years ago, any date is feasible, and to be honest, merely a secondary issue. These sins of omission of historians, anthropologists, and other commentators intrude into the lives of every Original Australian person who must suffer the misrepresentation that, until the whites came to Australia, nothing of worth was manufactured, discovered, or achieved. Irrespective of timing and potential exportation, very few are aware that these inventions and insights, plus so much more, all began in Australia.

CHAPTER 12

THE ORIGINS OF THE 4 R'S (READIN', 'RITIN', 'RITHMETIC, AND 'RT)

Whether or not the many Original Australian insights, skills, and refinements discussed in the previous chapter were actually exported abroad and absorbed into the fabric of societies throughout the globe can never be proven in absolute terms. As is the case with all interpretations of the distant past; they amount to an equation indicating degrees of possibility.

What is clear, however, is that the British invaders did not come seeking wisdom, culture, or civilization. They presumed that their empire represented the culmination of these, and the march of progress that began in Mesopotamia was set on the right path intellectually in Greece and spiritually in Rome—somewhat circuitously via "the Holy Land." The Europeans believed they already had all of the virtues of mind and spirit well in advance of the rest of the world. All they hoped to find in the new land were more resources to exploit, a geographically strategic position, and a place to house undesirables who would provide a cheap labor force.

Yet, even if they had come with open minds and hearts and some sense of humility, it would have been difficult for them to read all of the signs of the wisdom, culture, and ability of the Original inhabitants of their new possession. While much was, no doubt, deliberately ignored, probably even more was merely missed by those unable to read the clear signs before their very eyes. So the truth fell foul, not merely due to deliberate fabrication (as we shall see in our next chapter) but also due to the newcomers ignorance of the local language and inability to read the culture, art, and glyphs of the Original Australians.

We believe there is no better example of this incomprehension, and the violence it does to history, however unwittingly at times, than the commentary accompanying the photograph taken near the banks of the Coomera River towards the end of the nineteenth century. As we saw in the previous chapter, the photograph, now stored in the John Oxley Library, is supposed to be of "a large group of tribesmen spearing fish in the Coomera River."[1] We have already seen that it is not, and all that the photographer's observation shed light upon was how the inability to either communicate or empathize with people of a different tongue can muddy the waters.

Unable to speak the dialect, the photographer failed to perceive what was really happening and quite literally couldn't see the dolphins. Nor was he privy to a variety of reports of the same activity witnessed by magistrates and police which would have made clear what was really happening. Although there are no spears, this is a hunting party, but only half of the participants were captured by the lens—the ones without a dorsal fin. The Elder standing with arms stretched is obviously directing proceedings as he sings up the dolphins. The branches thrashed against the water alert their aquatic kin to their whereabouts, while the Elder's singing seeks approval and a communion very few will ever appreciate. The men remain stationary, their role being to stand in the shallowest area of the river, located where those who are pointing indicate, and quietly await further assistance and fleeing fish.

The rest was simply a matter of accepting nature's bounty: the dolphins would form a line and drive the school towards the men standing in the shallow water. The fish became stranded and, unable to swim backwards, were easily collected by the men in numbers enough for both tribes to share.

Unfortunately, according to the official notation and therefore history, this extremely important documentation of ritualized contact and cooperation between dolphins and humans has been relegated to the category of a day at the beach fishing. Typically, this is not merely the result of a lack of communication but yet another example of the distortion of history and denial of exceptional abilities that transcend those of the dominant culture. Equally, it also affirms the reality that without cultivating a common understanding, Original Australian sailors making contact with other peoples would not have been able to effectively dispense the gifts of esoteric teachings and guidance they bore.

Insofar as they succeeded in this, they must have made an effort of communication far greater than that of those who came to their shores in the eighteenth century. For the failure of the invader to understand was a result of their remaining ignorant of the culture of the local inhabitants in spite of it being clearly written for anyone who desired to learn how to recognize the script. Or perhaps we should cast that in the plural, for there were at least four types of text that would have gone some way toward breaching the communication divide: the spoken word, the glyph, the mathematical construction, and painting. It can be assumed that it was via a combination of at least some of these means of communication that the message of the Dreaming was spread throughout the world.

THE ENGRAVED WORD

There is a recognized ancient artistic style that is spread throughout Australia and is referred to as the Panaramitee tradition. What remains controversial is the meaning of these symbols and glyphs and the idea that any symbols found outside Australia derive from an Antipodean source.

Originally discovered in 1923, near Lake Eyre in South Australia, is an engraving of a crocodile. Not only is this a work of considerable artistic merit but also, according to eminent archaeologist Josephine Flood, "it may derive from a time where terrestrial crocodiles and humans actually co-existed in South Australia, although the youngest crocodiles found so far date to more than 75,000 years."[2]

Not only is that date close to 50,000 years earlier than any form of art found anywhere else in the world, but it is also far from an isolated instance of such activity. Also discovered at Panaramitee was another set of engravings which were dated by Dr. Donald Dorn, through assessing the cation ratio, to be older than 43,000 years old.

However, these ancient engravings are not merely crude illustrations of the local flora and fauna. They often take on the form of a narrative which those adept in ancient lore can most certainly read between the grooves of. Les Wilton, whose grandfather was one of the last to live a fully traditional life, learned all he could from his kin, and is one of the very few able to decipher these shapes and glyphs. One engraving at Olary (which is close to Panaramitee and of that style) has the outward appearance of four simple circles of varying diameters, with one line intersecting. In Les's eyes, it describes how three tribes argued with the fourth, with the group furthest to the right offending the other three, being therefore responsible for the dispute. In European eyes there are four circles and a line, end of story.

These ancient sites, and many others, bearing identical motifs and symbols are spread throughout the country, and led archaeologist Lesley Maynard to conclude that not only was this the oldest example of *Homo sapiens* art, but the base and origin upon which all forms of writing and grammar evolved. As expected, the prevailing conservative academic climate in Australia did not take kindly to such nonsensical notions, but fortunately one professor saw merit in Maynard's observation and came up with an ingenious, and slightly devious, ploy to assess the bona fides of Maynard's theory. Professor Bednarik sent photos of ancient glyphs inscribed into rocks, situated in Africa, the USA, and Europe, to suitably qualified scholars around the world. Bednarik deliberately excluded any photographs of Australian engravings from this portfolio. In what surely confirmed Maynard's suspicions, 98% of the respondents nominated the place of origin of all the photographs submitted to be Australia.

The results were so uniform, and percentages so large, Bednarik was left with two options. "It is either not possible to identify the Panaramitee style, or . . . this is a world-wide style."[3]

THE PAINTED WORD

The consensus amongst experts is that painting began in France. Whether the first evidence of this activity can be found at Lascaux or Aurignac is still a point of conjecture, but irrespective of specific locale, the oldest date attributed to any form of artistic endeavor outside Australia is 32,000 years.

However, the systematic use of ochre in Australia, to satisfy both artistic and spiritual needs, is much older than any date coming out of France. "Pieces of ochre, some showing clear striations from use, occur in most Pleistocene sites in Australia, including the lowest levels in Nauwalabila and Malakunanja II, first occupied before 50,000 BP."[4]

Of course the use of ochre was never restricted to the side of cave walls. Not only was painting rock a way of satisfying creative urges and religious obligations, the application of ochre on the body occurred throughout Australia for tens of thousands of years. As is the norm, the smearing of ochre onto skin first began in Australia. Accompanying the burial of WLH3, which was claimed to have occurred no less than 45,000 years ago, and quite probably more than 60,000 years ago, "the bones and surrounding sand was stained pink; the pink color, derived from ochre powder scattered over the corpse, clearly defined the size and shape of the grave."[5]

Red ochre is not merely a vibrant color that was used to decorate walls and skin, it is also recognized as the most sacred color of the Original Australians' palette. Irrespective of color or medium, the primary function of their art was to convey a message that was essentially spiritual. One must be careful not to confuse present-day uses of art with those of the ancient past. In many cases, traditional Australian art and religion were so intertwined they performed the same function. With the exception of the Panaramitee style, which was the foundation upon which all regional styles were inspired, until quite recently, each region exhibited one particular style that belonged to the people, tribal estate, and Creation Spirits of that place. It could neither be transferred nor altered, as it was a gift of the Gods. Acting as a central focus, artworks recorded oral myths and narratives for posterity and future ceremonies.

THE SPOKEN WORD

However, not just the syntax and symbols that underpin the engraved word and painted narrative were exported from Australia, but the actual spoken word is an integral part of this Ancient Australian legacy.

At the turn of the nineteenth century, the German anthropologist, Dr. Hermann Klaatsch, introduced the notion of on-field intensive study to the universities of Europe. To launch this radical concept, he embarked upon a three-year investigation (1904–1906) into the lives of traditional Australian people. Convinced it was from Australia modern man first evolved, and that it was therefore also the birthplace of art, religion, language, and the other foundation stones of true culture, he spent three years on the continent gathering evidence that he felt validated his theory.

Klaatsch was particularly taken by the striking similarities between many Original Australian dialects and European languages. What stood out, even more so for those whose native tongue was German, was the vocabulary of the Originals of Western Australia. So obvious were the links between the Original Australian and German language that the Lutheran missionaries were originally at a loss to fathom how this could be. Their explanation, as provided by Klaatsch, was naïve, but did serve to illustrate how strongly the two languages melded. He noted that "according to the missionaries it was the confusion of the tongues at the tower of Babel that cut off the ancestors of the Australians from other races."[6] This does not reveal a great deal of logical thinking on the part of the missionaries—for if the Original speakers had been cut off and the purity of the first language had been preserved with them, it makes the Germans' ability to communicate with them somewhat mysterious, unless their tongue was also supposed to date back to Babel. Nonetheless, Klaatsch explained why he included the idea in his commentary when remarking that as "childish as these ideas are, they are of value in some respects, as they give us an impartial testimony to the Indo-Germanic affinities to the Australians."[7]

It would be a mistake to assume this linguistic connection applies solely to the German language. Klaatsch was particularly interested in establishing a commonality between the most basic words. Simply because the need and frequency of the most pressing objects and basic emotions logically lead to a situation where these ideas and things would become the first words spoken. And it was here, at the most primal level, the links and precedence were strongest.

"The Latin *acqua*, the English 'water' (British and Irish 'usk,' and German 'wasser' etc) which remind us of the constantly repeated 'arra,' 'warra' and 'larra' of the Australian dialects . . . The word 'manda' (hand) for instance, is found over a large area, and recalls the Latin *manus* . . . Not less striking is the resemblance of 'bina' (ear, leaf, feather) to the corresponding Latin word *pinna*. In Queensland I found the word 'jepar' for liver, which in Greek is 'hepar': and Bradshaw, an authority on the Australians, gives 'kaputa' for 'head' (Latin *caput*) as used by a central Australian tribe."[8]

Even the Original place names adopted by the British offered up interesting parallels. Klaatsch noted that "there is a flourishing little town in New South Wales called Toowoomba (or Tuwumba) after a 'cucumber' (Latin *cucumba*) that grows in the district."[9] (The fact that Toowoomba is actually in Queensland across the border doesn't diminish the startling nature of the observation, though it does add an amusing twist to it.)

This small sampling is sufficient for our purposes, but slightly misleading in one regard. Klaatsch was focusing on confirming the undeniable affinities to European language (which he referred to as Indo-Germanic), while Professor A. P. Elkin wasn't seeking any linguistic link. He was having more than enough trouble making any meaningful verbal communication when he made a startling discovery. Elkin, who soon after he was appointed to chair the first Anthropology faculty at Sydney University, was trying to create understanding with the local people from the Kimberley region who had never made direct contact with any Europeans. After exhausting his large reservoir of neighboring dialects, the impasse was broken when these illiterate naked hunter-gatherers began "greeting him with Ancient secret masonic hand signs . . . many of the words spoken of Egyptian origin."[10]

Another fascinating linguistic connection is also evident in India. In his highly regarded book *Voices of the First Day*, Robert Lawlor noted, in regard to the speech of the people of southern India, "all of the Dravidian dialects are agglutinative, as are the Australian languages."[11] Of itself, the shared tendency to merge root words narrows the odds that the Australian Original tongue was the first language in India (and everywhere else), but Lawlor was even more specific. "The Dravidian fishermen of the Madras coast use almost the same words for *I, thou, he, we,* and *you* as some Aboriginal tribes. Many other key words in the Dravidian dialect are identical to Tasmanian Aboriginal terms in both pronunciation and meaning."[12]

THE FINAL COUNTDOWN

With the origins of readin', 'riting, and 'rt addressed, there still remains the fourth "r," 'rithmetic. One would expect, simply because, it is often claimed, Original Australian counting stops at four or five, this is the one academic field where looking somewhere else would be more fruitful. For many, math and numbers are synonymous, and assumed to be the core from which mathematics evolved.

But there is much more to mathematics than the manipulation of numbers to keep stock of personal assets, money, and sundry items. Geometry, angles, alignments, the classification of objects through the comparison of common qualities, and many other methods of estimation and arrangement should also be included under that umbrella.

As such, the recently discovered astronomical stone constructions found at Wurdi Youang (near Mt. Rothwell, Victoria) display an extremely ancient familiarity with a branch of mathematics which is essential for any voyagers crossing great expanses of ocean searching for new lands. A group of eminent scientists, led by astrophysicist Professor Ray Norris from the CSIRO, announced to the world that Original Australian "tribes carefully arranged rocks to map the progress of the sun 10,000 years ago."[13] The rock formation referred to was laid out in a semi-circle to precisely map the sun. The CSIRO scientists were adamant that, "this can't be done by guesswork"[14] and "required very careful measurements"[15] but more importantly, their calculations indicated an antiquity that none were expecting.

In their estimations, this device was constructed 10,000 years ago, and "predates the Egyptians, the Pyramids, Stonehenge, all that stuff."[16] According to all accepted versions of Australian pre-history, the existence of such activities necessitating "very careful measurement"[17] 10,000 years ago is not even on the radar, let alone in any approved text book. Nor is this discovery an isolated one. We are aware of an even more extensive and intricate astronomical construction that dwarfs these stone markers, of which the details will be shared in our next book. For now, let it suffice us to note that the deliberate placement of rocks and alignments created at Wurdi Youang are sufficient to establish the mathematical credentials of the Original Australians.

We have already seen how Original language may have contributed to many of the lexicons spread throughout the world. This may also extend to the language of math. When examining the most basic numbers, one and two, Hermann Klaatsch noted that. "These are found in all dialects . . . the words for one and two ('unnar' and 'djakala') have certain amount of resemblance to the Latin (*una* and *duo*)."[18]

It came as no surprise to Klaatsch that there were many variations of the most basic counting skills exhibited throughout Australia. "A particularly interesting chapter is the early history of the words and signs for numbers. Here we find the human hand once more in a new part—as a calculating apparatus: as it is still used by young, and often older, people. The Australian languages bring out the connection with the hand as clearly as Roman numerals do. The Roman V is clearly the outline of a hand with the thumb extended and the X represents two crossed hands."[19]

Of course, these connections through language are not found in isolation. As we have seen, the same story is repeated whether examining mitochondrial DNA, Y chromosomes, blood groupings, skull morphology, Dreaming stories, historical records, and accounts given by the custodians of ancient lore. It all began in Australia, and as reminded by an Elder versed in ancient lore, if "all other people of the world come from us"[20] then so, too, does language, religion, art, sailing, surgery, and the essential notions of gender equality and democracy. The rest is history.

CHAPTER 13

THE MYTH OF TERRA NULLIUS

Wednesday 22nd August 1770 . . . after we anchor'd we saw a
number of People upon this Island arm'd in the manner as all
others we have seen, except one man who had a bow and a
bundle of arrows, the first we have seen on this coast.[1]

When the British first made their unwelcome intrusion into the
great southern land, it was with few ideas of anything other than
their divine mandate to rule and confiscate at their leisure. The theft
of Australian land and destruction of the local inhabitants' dignity
contravened every international law. This was law of which the British authorities must have been well aware, and invasion could only
proceed through doing as much violence to the truth as they did to
the Original Australians. Every official report served the same pernicious purpose and was characterized by omission, selective recall,
and outright lies.

Even before Cook set sail, the Admiralty made it clear, officially
at least, that they were bound by convention and ethics. Lord Moreton, President of the Royal Society, gave Cook, Banks, and Solander
specific instructions in relation to if and when they may claim sovereignty and raise the flag. "They are the natural, and in the strictest
sense of the word, legal possessors of the several regions they inhabit.
No European nation has the right to occupy any part of their country,
or settle among them, without their voluntary consent."[2]

The crucial aspect, the two words upon which everything else
evolves and still does, was the demand to obtain "voluntary consent."[3]
That requirement was not negotiable, and a fundamental prerequisite for settlement and, without its fulfillment, whatever took place

could only be defined as a crime. From the moment the Union Jack was unfurled, in defiance of Moreton's strictures and all International Law, the British version of history has been tainted by alibis and fabrications. The truth was the first casualty of this illegal invasion.

Legal British settlement in Australia could only begin once there was agreement and compensation; this was obligatory. The Admiralty left no doubts or room to manipulate, and went to extraordinary lengths when emphasising the legal rights of the Original people of this land. Nonetheless, it was also clear from the instructions that the acquisition of new land was part of the purpose of the mission.

"You are also with the Consent of the Natives to take possession of Convenient Situations in the Country . . . or if you find the Country uninhabited take Possession for his Majesty . . ."[4]

Never did Cook, Banks, or any other witness deny the land was populated. Granted they may have grossly underestimated the numbers and intelligence of the inhabitants, but no one made claim to the land being vacant. Equally, Cook openly admitted no conversation took place, nothing was shared other than misgivings, and the only consent obtained was for safe passage when vacating tribal lands. Whether the emphasis British officialdom put upon gaining the consent of the existing inhabitants was due to international legal conventions or a sense of compassion is a moot point. Whatever the motive, the basic conventions of law were not observed.

Regardless of whether the colonizers sought to obtain land via negotiation or seek out unpopulated regions, it is clear that they knew significant tracts were inhabited. Even precluding the idea that there had been earlier secret British missions, this fact makes it clear that the British had extensive knowledge about this continent well before Cook set sail. With these pre-existing understandings evident, it would appear any British invading force could never be able to then claim the country was uninhabited.

Regardless of what actually took place, it is undeniable that "according to international law of Europe in the late 18th century, there were only three ways that Britain could take possession of another country.

"1. If the country was uninhabited, Britain could take possession by claiming and settling that country. In this case, Britain could claim ownership of the land and share it among its own people."[5]

For this possibility to apply, there could be no official record of pre-existing human settlement, such as a formal declaration of hostilities or any form of treaty would clearly indicate. If the concept of *Terra Nullius*—an unpeopled land—was to be invoked, the only organized group prepared for a fight could be themselves.

"2. If the country was already inhabited, Britain could ask for permission from the indigenous people to use some of their land. In this case Britain could purchase land for its own use but it could not steal the land of the indigenous people."[6]

Instructed to obtain "permission"[7] through negotiating the ownership of "some"[8] parcels of land, Cook's actions are in direct contravention to what his orders demand. With no payment made, permission sought, or negotiation taking place in a country with a population of no less than one million people, there was no mechanism for any British person to legally set foot in any nation inhabited by the Original Australians. Without a solitary treaty, financial recompense, or even an illiterate cross scrawled on a piece of paper, Cook's actions when hoisting the flag and claiming ownership of massive tracts of land over which the British had jurisdiction have no legality whatsoever.

The third form of colonial theft, and obviously the path of greatest resistance and least morality, was to lay claim to Australia through conquest. But this does carry with it an obligation to recognize prior presence and legal possession.

"3. If the country was inhabited, Britain could take over the country by invasion and conquest—in other words, defeat that country in war."[9]

The invasion of another people's territory, to be legally concluded, involves some form of treaty being signed, and thus, the legal existence of the invaded party is acknowledged. If there were two nations at war, any pretense that the doctrine of *Terra Nullius* applied could not be maintained. The reality was that, for the first fifteen years the Europeans and Original Australians were at war. Twice the invading soldiers, first the French and then the British, retreated in battle, giving up close to half of their fleet or garrison to the local warriors. The British did indeed invade a settled continent, and make war on a people who had deliberately kept apart and caused no other nation any grief. But when such an event occurs, we must have an acknowledgment of habitation, which has only recently been granted, and a treaty, which still hasn't.

With these agreed European parameters in operation, it was assumed the race between colonial powers to steal and invade would be a civilized contest between honorable gentlemen honoring the rights of the traditional inhabitants. But in this case even the façade of justice was sacrificed and the British had no pose of legal validity to fall back upon. Not only the politicians, but the educated citizens of Britain knew the proposed 1788 expedition to Australia was both illegal and guaranteed to inflict great suffering upon the rightful custodians of the land. Two letters written to the editors of the *London Morning Herald* and *London Morning Chronicle* by concerned citizens are quite prophetic in sharing the same fears and tragedies they foresaw once the fleet hoisted anchor.

One correspondent, concerned about "the transportation of felons to Botany Bay," believed nothing good would eventuate. They despaired that "those, therefore, who are the pests of society in this country, are to be favored with a settlement in a much more delightful region than that from which they are removed; and the natives because they are justly and naturally jealous of such invasion, must be destroyed by the armed force which is sent out with the convicts, to support occupancy of lands not their own."[10]

Not only was this invasion fleet manned with what the respectable members of society regarded as its dregs, it was guaranteed to "strike panic"[11] and had the makings of something far worse. "I hope the English annals will never be stained with shedding innocent blood,"[12] the missive writer notes, somewhat in vain, before concluding with a prophetic and ominous contemplation: "will they at all benefit a race of men who are content with the spot nature has allotted them; whose wants are few and whose virtue, perhaps, exceeds our capacity for thinking . . ."[13]

Here we have one correspondent living on the opposite side of the globe, who had never seen an inhabitant of Australia, yet was able to intuit, in his speculation, that their "virtue, perhaps, exceeds our capacity for thinking."[14] This missive highlights a liberal sentiment among the more enlightened members of British society, of which Phillip was acutely aware. He was, therefore, fully cognizant of the fact that the settlers' actions within this new frontier would be rigorously scrutinized, and that official reports of events taking place in Australia could create controversy and embarrassment for his masters if the true situation was known. Talk of massacre, murder, conflict, and moral degradation was something Phillip had to avoid at all costs.

Well before the First Fleet sailed out of British waters, the official history of first contact was already written. To be more precise, it wasn't so much what was written, but the omissions that were bound to follow and the censorship of all official correspondence. There would be no account of organized resistance or justified complaint, and no "natives"[15] would be shot unless under the most extreme provocation. Whatever actually occurred after arrival was incidental at best. The plot, scenes, and conclusion were penned in another country in advance, in defense of a land-theft of unparalleled dimensions, and in absolute defiance of both International Law and the spirit of the Dreaming. Phillip, as Governor-General, had to be vigilant in ensuring an appropriately sanitized and highly selective version of the truth reached the home front.

However, omission alone was insufficient with the morals of their more humane citizens and the conventions of International Law standing in the way. Something else was needed to tip the scales of opinion and vindicate the theft of an entire continent. Public sentiment had to be massaged to counter the unmistakeable reality of crime being crime, and this could only be achieved by creating the perception that nothing of worth was being stolen. What if one party was totally debased and primitive, and possibly not fully human, stagnating in a technology of sticks and stones? What if they lacked any transcendent wisdom and had hitherto been devoid of the benevolent guidance that only the inheritors of the wisdom of Greece and Rome could supply? Could such fabrications provide a legal justification when none existed?

Any perusal of the administration's correspondence coming out of the colony at the time would suggest this is so. Official reports often bore testimony to an undeserving population who were incapable of harvesting nature's bounty through agriculture. Bereft of clothing and shame, lacking in permanent monuments, books, buildings, or economy, these people were soon regarded as a lesser species; somewhat akin to a primitive human genetic cul-de-sac doomed to stagnate in its inferiority. How could a culture without a class system know anything of nobility? Living under the stars without the protection of walls and the collection of taxes to build them, they were more like animals than people. Without the rudiments of literacy, no treaty could be signed, even if the new lords of the land thought that the right of habitation should be granted to people so undeserving. They would not even make good serfs and were therefore relegated to a class below that of the peasant.

The Original Australians, therefore, came to occupy a nebulous legal category, in that they existed in every sense and were protected by every law, including those of the British, and yet were invisible and dispossessed in the actual reality of being nominated part of a British colony. Their continent was, somewhat bewilderingly, proclaimed to be subject to the legal embrace of *Terra Nullius*. Not because the continent was uninhabited—because even the British knew this was untrue and unsustainable in any court—but simply due to the Original Australians' perceived inability to fence, farm, or write. Their status was not derived through considering what they had achieved—for as we saw in the last chapter, even if the invader had wished to perceive this, they did not have the eyes with which to see. Rather, their virtue was measured by what was absent and, thereby, they lost all rights and legal standing due to this being considered the standard of inferiority.

This image of the local people being heavily promoted, there is no surprise that the popular conception came to be that the race needed to be re-educated, civilized, and Christianized. They would have to be taught the benefits of clothing, agriculture, and housing. Their souls would be purged of all Satanic primal influences and their minds freed from the yokes of superstition and pagan primitivism. Obviously, in this transitionary phase, those with fairer skin and a more refined nature were virtually compelled to farm the land, develop the resources, and control the destiny of the lesser beings they had conquered.

Banks was certainly one of many who subscribed to this extreme form of paternalism though openly admitting he understood very little in regards to the culture or people. He made no attempt to breach this divide, but in spite of this paucity of knowledge was content to present himself to the British Parliament in 1785 as an expert.

"Question: Do you think that 500 men put on the shore there would meet with any obstruction from the natives which might prevent them settling there?

"Joseph Banks: Certainly not—from the experience I have had of the natives of another part of the same coast I am inclined to believe that they would speedily abandon the country of the newcomers."[16]

We find it quite galling any notice was taken of Banks, especially so when the question that followed his prognostications on how Originals would respond to an armed invasion force reveals absolutely nothing. He admits to having no understanding of Original organizations, customs, or language.

"Question: Have you any idea as to the nature of Government under which they lived?

"Joseph Banks: None whatsoever, nor their language."[17]

Armed with an appreciation of Original politics and language that amounted to "none whatsoever" and motivated by despotism and theft, every British colonial authority was aware they could only afford good news to leave the colony, whatever its relation to the truth might be. And it was for this reason that most history books state that the first four years of colonization were characterized by the good intentions of Phillip and harmonious relations with the locals. Their interaction was assumed to be cordial, and in the case of the Elder, Bennelong, verging on empathetic.

Or so one story goes, but, as we shall see, there is another version of events outside Phillip's PR machine. The personal recollection of his subordinate officers tell another tale altogether. For, although the official version of history is largely a net of lies woven by the conquerors, an occasional minnow of truth slips through the mesh. Despite their testimony, even though Phillip is exposed as a habitual liar in every word his quill penned, to this day the governor's version still prevails. Even the most cursory comparison between Phillip's official version and the entries made in the diaries/journals of Watkin-Tench, Captains Bradley and Collins, Lieutenant William Dawes, and others reveals two diametrically opposed interpretations of the same event. Someone is clearly lying, and identifying the culprit doesn't take a Sherlock Holmes.

Nor need we pretend to have much work to do, personally, in that regard as the case has already been skillfully tried in *The Myth of Terra Nullius,* and we could not do better than to borrow extensively from that excellent book. Somehow, this insightful publication, for a brief time, slipped past the censor's attention and was released through NSW high schools as an approved text. But not for long—apart from the first very limited release, no more texts were sent to schools and no further mention or recommendation was made.

"Governor Phillip is talking about the same event, but he leaves out some information"[18] . . . "Governor Phillip leaves out some information and creates a different impression of the same event"[19] . . . "It is interesting that Governor Phillip did not report about his party shooting"[20] . . . "How does Bradley's report contradict Governor Phillip's report"[21] . . . "There are other occasions when Governor

Phillip's reports were different to the reports made by people who witnessed the same events."[22]

Given this testimony, it does not take a Queen's Counsel to identify the ramblings of a habitual liar. But before casting too many aspersions upon Phillip's character, it needs to be acknowledged that those the governor served made it incumbent upon him to concoct such fabrications. Government documents could not be allowed to detail murder and wars of invasion carried out against an innocent nation in defiance of their sovereign rights.

Nonetheless, when one examines accounts which differ wildly in their details, Phillip's rendition portrays himself behaving somewhat like a Messianic figure whose primitive adversaries literally fall to their knees in supplication before him. This self-deification seems to go somewhat further than merely satisfying the needs of political expediency. Throughout Phillip's fabrications there was no mention of orchestrated acts of defiance, no talk of dispute or retaliation, any more than there was an admission of murder through musket.

The actions of the convicts were a different issue and one he always kept at arm's length: his rationale being the criminals were of a coarser disposition and any conflict reported was due to their ignorant state. But if the musket was fired, the army could only do so in defense when under attack and then the skirmish had to be downgraded from armed resistance to "an incident," from a dispute between a sovereign nation and an invading power, to a squabble between savages and criminals, both of which the long-suffering noble men of England were burdened with. Once an official declaration of hostilities was made public, then the official existence of an enemy would be recognized and the claim of the British on their territory would have to be defended, which it could not be by the rules of International Law the British gave lip service to.

We suspect the desire to compete in this illegal course of acquisition was incentive enough for the French ships, which arrived within weeks of Phillip, to set anchor, step ashore, and establish a substantial camp at a site which was named after the captain-in-charge of this naval expedition: La Perouse. What their long-terms goals were, and how long they intended to stay, are facts that are both obscure. We cannot know, in fact, if they would have indeed stayed had circumstances not altered so drastically. Of course, this is all supposition, for once the French made the mistake of behaving "very ill to some of the natives,"[23] they were left with only one choice: to raise anchor and set sail.

An account of the battle that saw the French boats and sailors retreat and abandon one of their boats to the local warriors was provided by a British sailor—Newtown Fowell—who was "told the story by the French sailors who were attacked on that day."[24]

"The natives before were very friendly to them and at this time one of the boats was aground and when they came down to murder them the French supposed their intent was to assist them with launching the boat that was aground. It was supposed that upwards of 500 stones was thrown in the first shower.

"The French immediately discharged a volley of small arms at them and it is supposed above 20 of the natives must have been killed—several of the French were also wounded. Those who escaped swam off to their other boat which lay off a small distance. The reason for this we could not learn.

"The French at first say'd they supposed (the attack) must have been for the sake of keeping the boats, but afterwards some hints dropt that it was one of their sailors had behaved very ill to some of the natives."[25]

With over "500 stones thrown"[26] in "the first shower"[27] of battle, twenty "natives"[28] dead and "several"[29] of their own wounded, this was a major confrontation. Moreover, so great was the danger, the French fled and abandoned one of the only three boats they had to the Australian warriors. This encounter marks the first of many that took place over the next fifteen years. It is quite possible, the next time the French set foot anywhere near this section of land nothing good would come from it, and with Port Jackson taken by the British, this open display of warfare was ample incentive to leave. For whatever reason, the French departed, and once they did, it would appear all issues relating to legitimacy and rights of conquest sailed off into the distant horizon.

Equally, from that day onwards, there could only be one sanctioned version of daily events and one person entrusted to record what happened and who was responsible. Phillip was now sole arbitrator, scribe, and judge, and his word was final.

Even the first sighting and the minutes before they set foot on Australian soil are a matter of dispute and subject to widely diverging accounts. Watkin-Tench was immediately aware of how Cook had grossly underestimated the number of natives, and the imminent danger they now faced. The final location for the landing-party was selected solely due to it being the least dangerous. It was certainly made clear their presence was unwelcomed.

"Even at the harbor's mouth we had reason to conclude the country more populous than Mr. Cook thought it. For on the Supply's arrival in the Bay on the 18th of the month, there were assembled on the beach of the south shore, to the number not less than forty persons, shouting and making uncouth signs and gestures as prudence forbade a few people to venture among so great a number, and a party of only six men was observed on the north shore, the Governor immediately proceeded to land on that side, in order to take possession of his new territory, and bring about an intercourse between old and new masters."[30]

It is a shame the "new masters"[31] assumed they could simply "take possession"[32] and that some formal form of "intercourse"[33] would automatically ensue. It is obvious their lives were at risk, and that Phillip's choice of landing site was predicated upon selecting the least threatening. However, in Phillip's account the natives were compliant and in utter awe of the British's arrival, and in particular Phillip's personality. As he walks alone among these agitated savages refusing to relinquish arms, they literally fall to their knees in supplication in deference to his heroic presence. And of course, amidst whatever news from the colonies did reach British shores, there would be no mention of "dispute."[34] What we do find is a first-person account littered in personal pronouns, a sizeable ego, and blatant disregard for the truth:

"When I first landed in Botany Bay the natives appeared on the beach, and were easily persuaded to receive what was offered them, and, tho' they came armed, very readily returned the confidence I placed in them, by going to them alone and unarmed, most of them laying down their spears when directed; and while the ships remained in Botany Bay no dispute happened between our people and the natives."[35]

Despite the self-serving spin Phillip puts on his gloss of the situation, may we suggest that, if they had landed on the "south shore,"[36] nothing more would have been heard from Phillip, Watkin-Tench, or any of the landing party. Philip's version contradicts not only the hostile atmosphere of first contact, but simply fictionalizes his role. He would have us believe that, by the sheer natural superiority of his nature, Philip strides into this potentially explosive situation and, by virtue of his magnificence diffuses the potential for conflict. Apparently, most of the naked warriors bowed to his will and bravery and voluntarily disarmed. Once his eminence had been established, or so one version claims, all of the natives were pacified (which must also include the "uncouth"[37] larger tribe they avoided in Botany Bay) and peace reigned.

The next incident again consists of two contradictory reports. However, this time it is not Watkin-Tench's report which challenges Phillip's honesty; the opposing testimony is sourced from the journal of Lieutenant William Bradley. On this occasion, on Phillip's orders, shots were fired in response to a trifling indiscretion. Undeniably Phillip's intention to kill would have drawn the displeasure of many in England, but only if news of this conflict was reported in a truthful fashion.

Phillip and Bradley were sailing in Botany Bay during March, 1788, when the weather took a sudden turn for the worse. A *Guringai* Elder "helped Phillip and his men land their boats and find shelter from a storm."[38] Once they were settled and sheltered, the Elder left them and claimed a shovel as payment for his services. According to Bradley, Phillip reacted in an extremely violent and provocative fashion that was guaranteed to create an ominous precedent and long-term repercussions.

"Sunday 8 PM: After dark the old man took an iron spade and was going off with it, he was seen from the longboat, pursued and brought back with it . . . The governor chastised him for it, which so enraged him that he ran off and very soon returned with his party all with their spears ready to throw, when a musket was fired which made them stop and a second musket drove them away for the night."[39]

Not only is Phillip stingy in not paying for services rendered, but, once his quill is in his hand, one can be assured that no musket was raised. However, if danger does present itself, the Governor will stand tall and simply through his steely glare and firm countenance resolve the impasse without a shot fired or spear thrown:

"When it was dark he stole a spade, and was caught in the act. I thought it necessary to show that I was displeased with him, and therefore, when he came to me, pushed him away, and gave him two or three slight slaps on the shoulder with the open hand, at the same time pointing to the spade. This destroyed our friendship in a moment, and seizing a spear he came close up to me, poised it, and appeared determined to strike, but whether from seeing his threats were not regarded—for I chose rather to risk the spear than to fire on him . . . after a few minutes he dropped his spear and left us."[40]

What a selfless gesture! Phillip claims he was prepared to lay down his life rather than fire upon this enraged thieving primitive. The instructive value of the "slight slaps"[41] was somehow missed by the native miscreant who was unreasonable enough to take offense and devolve into a savage rage. Yet, rather than imperil the maintenance of political harmony, the governor refrained from firing a single shot that might destroy the accord he had won. Having utilized his normal modus operandi of laughing off death, this British superman stares down his foe for "a few minutes"[42] to send yet another native scampering off into the bush.

Watkin-Tench must have been aware of what the official line was, how all correspondence must be framed, and what must be omitted. Yet despite this, his record reveals that the scale of the conflict far exceeded anything his superior hinted at.

"Like ourselves the French found it necessary more than once, to chastise a spirit of rapine and intrusion which prevailed among Indians around the Bay."[43]

If this statement seems less than an outright admission of injustice, the same cannot be said of Bradley's testimony which concedes that innocents were shot by British and French soldiers.

"The musket seems the only thing that keeps them in awe . . . That some of them have been killed by musket balls, both at Port Jackson by our people and at Botany Bay by the French, I have not the least doubt."[44]

If, as Bradley was convinced, soldiers fired upon the Original Australians, then Phillip is either lying or incompetent.

When providing details of the battle at La Perouse, and in particular the tactics both sides employed, British sailor Newton Fowell is openly dismissive of the official line. Knowing full well both invading countries were equally guilty of the indiscriminate use of the musket, he concluded his correspondence with this question:

"How many people did British soldiers shoot without the officers writing it in their reports?"[45]

The answer would have been clear to everyone in the new colony, even if no one knew exact figures or cared to know. Such statistical questions can no longer be answered with any accuracy. Yet it is clear that a monstrous crime was committed, and the exact body count is hardly important, for it is not as if there is an acceptable level of genocide. Many of the traditional custodians of the land were shot dead during the early months and years after the invasion began, and policy must have been to avoid recording the fatalities. The Eora and surrounding tribes were defending their lands and fighting an undeclared war with the Europeans. It was for this reason the French departed after being defeated at the Battle of La Perouse. However, the three French boats and crew were an easy foe compared to the

British Fleet. Its sailors, officers, convicts, and Marine Corps were greater in number, better armed, and a much more formidable foe for warriors armed with sticks and stones.

Lieutenant William Dawes was a man of unusual compassion who displayed a genuine empathy and respect towards the Original Australians. He was the first to learn the Eora tongue, and when in conversation with one of their woman, whose name was Patyegarang, once again the topic of the musket and the reality of how often it was used reappeared. He was trying to determine why a white settler "had been wounded,"[46] and in particular, what offense triggered that response.

> Patyegarang: Gulara (Because they are angry).
> Dawes: Many-in gulara yura eora? (Why are the black men angry?)
> Patyegarang: Inyam ngala-wi whiteman. (Because the white men are settled here.)
> Dyaran Garmari-gai (The kamaragals are afraid.)
> Dawes: Miny-in tyarun kamaragal? (Why are the kamaragal afraid?)
> Patyegarang: Gan-in (Because of) the guns.[47]

No matter when or where early contact took place, it was made clear the invaders were unwelcome. At best they were tolerated for a limited duration, but Captain Collins had no trouble in breaching the divide in language and immediately learned the meaning of one word that echoed throughout Eora lands.

"The Governor set off on Monday the 21st, accompanied by Captain Hunter, Captain Collins, [etc] with a small party of marines for their protection, the whole being embarked in three open boats.

"Their little fleet attracted the attention of several parties of the natives, as they proceeded along the coast, who all greeted them in the same words, and in the same tone of vociferation, shouting everywhere 'Warra, warra, warra,' words which by the gestures that accompanied them, could not be interpreted into invitations to land, or expressions of welcome."[48]

Yet, when Phillip, seated alongside Collins, records the event, these overt displays of belligerence are minimized, and the local warriors soon acquiesce and meekly accept whatever is deemed appropriate. Apparently Phillip could see through this aggressive front and called their bluff. With his august presence at the helm, almost immediately they realized they were confronted by their superiors. He does concede there was an original reluctance to bond, but this is merely a temporary hindrance, and once he walked amongst them, their fears evaporated.

"When I first went in the boats to Port Jackson the natives appeared armed near the place at which we landed, and were very vociferous, but, like the others, easily persuaded to accept what was offered."[49]

Like errant schoolchildren in need of a firm but kind hand, Phillip continues in this account when describing another instance of benevolent contact at Manly Cove. This was one of the infrequent times where Phillip admitted to having to negotiate some "troublesome"[50] behavior, but fortunately "their curiosity"[51] when watching the British prepare food was under the watchful eye of Phillip. Once he stepped in and put the natives in their place, the primitive throng became compliant and "very quiet."[52]

Even though fully armed and the cause of considerable concern, "as their curiosity made them very troublesome when we were preparing our dinner, I made a circle around us. There was little difficulty in making them understand that they were not to come within it, and they sat down very quiet."[53]

Alas, when the Original Australians adopted the same strategy to delineate which areas the English could enter, they, to the contrary, did indeed experience some difficulty communicating their wishes.

However, it would be a mistake to presume the musket and uniform caused the Originals the greatest grief. It was the convicts and Phillip's leniency that were most responsible for the deterioration in relations. The prison walls were made from eucalypt and isolation, but within the confines of Sydney, they were free to wander as they saw fit and take whatever was freely available. The problem being, the notion of stealing—of taking canoes, nets, spears, and sundry utensils that were left at the place that was the most convenient—though an exotic concept to the Original Australians was second nature to the settlers. The convicts, and others, were more than willing to help themselves to whatever they came upon. So rampant was the practice, even though Phillip pleaded that the theft of property should cease, it continued until the *Eora* nation and people vanished.

"For the first three years, Governor Phillip usually blamed the convicts for any fights that occurred between the newcomers and Koori people."[54]

The convicts resented Phillip's attempt to put the blame for poor relations onto them. While it is hard to believe that the Original Australians would not have resented the presence of the invaders, regardless of their manners, there is no doubt that the character of the convicts added to the tension of the situation. While Phillip's casting aspersions upon his charges' righteousness may have been largely a matter of diminishing his own responsibility for the lack of harmony, it cannot be denied that the convicts were reported to have been behaving appallingly by other individuals.

Judge Collins, who had to deal with assessing the defense pleas of convicts charged with offending Eora men and women, remarked that, "it was . . . difficult to believe them."[55] Such a precarious relationship inevitably led to an exacerbation of the climate of conflict and the spilling of more of the blood of the innocent Original Australians.

The reality was this was a war, prosecuted by an ambitious and disrespectful British invasion force upon an innocent community who had never caused offense to any other nation on earth. The British neither appreciated nor respected the Original Australians who did everything humanly possible to repel their enemy. Not only were their tools and weapons being stolen, the British were virtually stealing the food out of their mouths.

Phillip admitted their "dislike of the Europeans is probably increased by discovering that they intend to remain among them, and that they interfere with them in some of their best fishing places, which doubtless are, in their circumstances objects of very great importance."[56]

The settlers were obviously unwelcome, which is hardly surprising as they were blatantly stealing food, tribal estates, goods, and chattels, while murdering any who objected. In short, all vestiges of morality were sacrificed in this institutionalized process of grand theft. As each day passed, relations deteriorated, but with the British in control of the muskets and the quill, it would appear there was little that could be done beyond accepting the plunder and waiting at the margins for death. Justice, if it was to be had, would clearly come in another world, presuming the British did not rule there, too, and Phillip was not truly the avatar of the Most High he presented himself to be.

Yet, with Pemulwuy leading the armed resistance, this war was nowhere near complete, and at Toongabbie with half the troopers in retreat and cowering behind the walls of a wooden garrison, praying the warriors under his leadership would not set the town and themselves alight, the war had only just began. However, it is beyond the scope of this book to follow the rest of this history through all its phases, and for that tragic story we direct the reader elsewhere.[57]

Let us suffice it here to note that armed resistance was eventually crushed, but it can be maintained that the war did not end once the Original Australians ceased to be openly hunted like so much game, at least not on the part of the invader. The open brutality of armed conflict merely gave way to a more insidious kind of attrition, marked by cultural genocide, suppression, exploitation, deaths in custody, the diaspora of the Stolen Generation, and all of the other shameful aspects that mark the history of white Australia's treatment of the Original Australians.

As to whether the lack of recognition of worth, denial of conflict, theft of country and purpose is any less painful than when the British first came is debatable, but there is a change at hand and talk of the completion of a cycle which the Ramindjeri nation of South Australia call *Wirritjin*, which means Black-fella White-fella Dreaming.

They believe, along with many others, the past is not lost, and will return.

How, why, and when this transformation will be achieved can only be answered by the custodians of culture, and can only be revealed if standing on country, with song, and under the guidance of men and women who refuse to sacrifice their culture and heritage for thirty pieces of silver.

CONCLUSION

Clearly this book can only act as a general introduction to the question of where *Homo sapiens* originated and the likelihood that it was on the continent we call Australia among the Original inhabitants of that land. So too, the question of what they might have taken with them is only partially covered, and only ongoing study and discovery will continue to build our picture of just how complex and sophisticated the culture and technology of the Original Australians was. The discovery of a single skull is enough to suggest evidence of trepanning and that of a single set of footprints hints strongly at a skill in amputation. No doubt there is much more that will be uncovered in the future to support or challenge these ideas.

Equally clearly, as the "political" part of our thesis makes clear, to date the invaders' understanding of the world of the Original People, its intrinsic value, and what it has to offer to the rest of the world shows severe limitations. As our last chapter shows, since the time of Cook and Phillip, little respect or serious consideration has been given to the actual accomplishments of the Original people: what little of it was recognized. This assumption that hunter-gatherer societies are "primitive" introduces a perception bias which mitigates against clear thinking and perceptive observation. While there has clearly been an improvement in this regard, gradually over a period of more than two centuries, we are still far from the sort of Copernican revolution that is required to make a real advance in thinking and achieve a sophisticated understanding of this area of inquiry.

Rather than the subject being primitive, it has been the understanding that was and largely continues to be so. Here, of course, there are exceptions. For every million flat-earthers or geocentrists there is an Aristarchus, a Kepler, or Copernicus at a certain time in history; those who live as heretics and sometimes also die as such, but not before they have been able to sway a certain number of thinkers to their cause, until a tipping point is met and the old heresy becomes the new orthodoxy.

The paradigm shift we hope to play our own small part in faces great challenges in a world where the iPhone is the closest thing to an icon we have. Where academic experts seem more interested in shoring up their reputations than the truth, regardless of how much evidence is presented for them to ignore. Where respect given to thinkers and researchers outside their cosily funded insular citadels of learning is scant.

If the proponent of an academically unorthodox view is an Original Australian Elder or some other person honored within a particular community, then, sometimes, a little more respect is forthcoming. Yet it is that of political correctness, rather than a genuine desire to even consider the possibility that someone outside the circles of enshrined learning might have valuable knowledge and insights. Knowledge and insights that, not only do they lack, but that they cannot acquire independently.

It should be clear by now that our approach is diametrically opposed to this. If we are in any sense trailblazers, it is not in revealing anything much in the way of new ideas, but more in terms of attempting to gain recognition for the knowledge and wisdom that has been available for an age, if one would only seek it with the right attitude of respect toward its custodians. The Elders of the Original Australians, who are the custodians not only of the land but also of the Dreaming, are our guides. We have also tried to honor and publicize the findings of those brave souls in the academic world and outside it who are willing to follow the evidence wherever it leads them and whatever the cost; who allow their presumptions to be challenged and their ideas to evolve in the true spirit of scientific inquiry.

Most of our observations serve as a brief summary of topics and issues already covered in far greater detail elsewhere, but even in this abridged form, the facts, history, and religious traditions we have presented in support of our belief the First Australians were the first *Homo sapiens sapiens* openly contradict every variation of the Out-of-Africa theory. These ideas should be given due consideration because they harmonize with what the Australian Original custodians of lore and history insist to be true.

Past this point we have nothing further to add, and even though we have barely scratched the surface in either complexity or scope, questions and inconsistencies in relation to the Out-of-Africa theory still remain, and an alternative explanation and location do exist.

However, before and during the time these articles were being written, there always was a more intriguing agenda demanding our attention. Far more important than any issue/proposition raised in this book are the secret stories revealed by Ramindjeri Elder and keeper of lore, Karno Walker. These were originally intended to be the final chapter. Then a senior park ranger sought us out with news of dates and massive astronomical constructions that not only confirmed one of the more sensational claims made by Karno, but ultimately put the final nail in the Out-of-Africa theory's coffin. The two stories were so intertwined and, as each day passed, have taken so many twists and turns they have become the principal areas to which our next book will be dedicated.

Our two sources are highly respected and would never lie about culture or lore, and it is our honor to be granted access to ancient stories and constructions that were deliberately kept secret, until now. Over the last few months we have heard talk of ancient Original mariners circumnavigating the world in a figure eight; the remains of Viking ships; an axe claimed to be over 100,000 years old; massive stone walls, some running parallel and others shaped like a trapezoid, marking out the paths of the sun, moon, planets, and other celestial objects; the largest engraved astrological chart in the world, the "Blue University"; a Wandjina gallery near Sydney and other sites that all contradict every conventional historical expectation.

For some who feel threatened by the change in historical precedence we propose, there has been a conditioned response of either refusing to look at or denigrating any hypothetical involvement of

Original Australians in ancient global affairs. At best, delegated to the status of a dubious historical possibility, the defenders of the status quo are quick to point out the economic advantages of the many conveniences and labor-saving devices some are privileged to own, and can see no practical benefit in mulling over yesterday's events.

For many in Western societies, the roots and structure of their institutions appear to have evolved out of ancient Greek civilization. The beginnings of science and medicine, the principles behind education, the very notion of democracy, all of this and much more that has been absorbed into the fabric of a variety of so-called democratic nations. But one must be wary, for it is a self-serving selection, more hypocrisy than Hippocrates. And while this diet of deceptions may cater to the appetite for acquisition that seems to dominate the "civilized world" to the soul, it is a Spartan ration of bread and water.

Plato, often regarded as the founding father of democracy, was ever vigilant in alerting others to the danger of forming a plebiscite and sharing power with a wider base. He felt any structure, no matter how egalitarian, was ultimately dependent upon the quality and sophistication of those who this society serves. If uncultured, uncouth, and unaware, it makes no difference what form of governance evolves, as the foundation is permanently decayed. Particularly evident in his many works portraying the ideas of his own Elder, Socrates, was Plato's revulsion towards two occupations: sophistry and cooking. Sophism's modern-day equivalents, politics and acting, were held in the lowest regard by Socrates, simply because both occupations depend more on delivery than actual knowledge of the subject matter. In these "arts," charisma and vocal inflection are qualities of the highest order, and an intimate understanding of the subject area is merely an added bonus, but certainly not essential. Equally, the popularity of cooking shows, often embellished with a competitive edge, seems to have no boundaries and an automatic guarantee of high ratings. The importance given to these three arenas of activity, according to Socrates, is the antithesis of what is required to nurture a knowledgeable and discerning electorate. Any regime, if founded upon a glib tongue, chocolate cakes, and superficiality, is doomed to fall. Socrates was adamant that democracy could only flourish within a political structure that nurtured the cultivation of the intellect and soul of all of its citizens.

Today, the social norms in Australia, specifically many that apply to men, stand in direct opposition to what Socrates would consider to be in harmony with any functioning democracy. Over thirty years ago, there was a series of four semi-fictional stories shown on the ABC network called *Women of the Sun* with Original Australian themes. The first episode dealt primarily with traditional life and contained a scene that typifies the chasm between cultures. In one scene the women sat together discussing the desirable qualities of prospective partners. What was noteworthy was the attributes they sought. There was no mention of wealth, ownership, prowess in any sport, persuasive tongue, political ambition, or skill with a hot plate. The qualities these women sought in a potential spouse related to their skills in dance, art, or hunting.

Apart from hunting, which is not a career path open to many contemporary "white" Australians, these other pursuits are most likely to be considered as signs of an unwelcome effeminacy or impracticality or both and something to be indulged in only by those willing to contemplate a modest if not impoverished life. To dance and create are not considered the prerogative of all but, rather, the province of an eccentric few. The career paths most desired by men seeking material comfort demand that the applicant is skilled in the fields of accountancy, oratory, and mathematics. The dancer and artist, with very few exceptions, are destined to struggle to survive in any society where the dollar rules.

Granted, prowess in sport is the modern-day equivalent to hunting, and something which many young Australian men desire. However, unless they are highly skilled and, therefore, financially rewarded, as the years pass, many men abandon the playing field for the lounge chair. The churches stand empty after shunning the Dreaming that might have provided it with new roots and real power. There can be little doubt that the chief deity in the modern world is Mammon, whose priesthood are the CEOs and whose temples are the corporate towers and the casinos. Everywhere, life seems so devoid of real meaning and pleasure that the anodyne of alcohol is the main remedy for making it bearable, with pornography another popular salve. The desire to create, to think, and seek the truth is replaced by an appetite for sensation, blockbuster fantasy, trivia, and gossip.

Time after time, when raising the issue of what has been lost in ignorance of the legacy of the Original Australians, the response has been as predictable as it is ominous: it is yesterday's news; we can't go back and must continue surging forward. Towards what? If running towards a cliff, there is no earthly reason to jump unless one is a lemming, yet humanity seems to show little more intelligence when it comes to blindly following in the footsteps of those in front. If, as Socrates warned, a worthwhile democracy can only be the end result of a caring, empathetic population, intelligent enough to independently determine right and wrong, then what we have today, marching on under the banner of an egalitarian democratic system, is a sham.

The quality of true leadership seems to have disappeared. Few politicians offer any real policy or vision and chop and change in an attempt to gauge the public whim and promise whatever will satisfy it, while doing what they planned with scant regard for how the two coincide. The populace, pacified with bread and circuses and distracted by shiny objects, have been convinced that they have chosen their slavery and to call it freedom. This is the glowing example held out to Indigenous peoples around the world for them to embrace. This is the gift they have received in return for the theft of their land and the denigration of their culture.

The truth is that democracy began in Australia, and remained dominant throughout the world until the advent of the plow and currency. The idea flickered momentarily in ancient Greece and then remained dormant until the nineteenth century. The problem is that the latest incarnation of this political system is rapidly reaching its expiry date, simply because its first allegiance is to the economy, not to the people.

The main reason defenders of the present capitalist system carp that we must continue consuming and moving forward is because any reversion to the original democratic model formed in the Dreaming is a path with lower company profits and a truly egalitarian goal. It is those roots, predicated upon cooperation and equality, which has been discarded for a more aggressive predatory approach where the survival of the fittest, whether on the battlefield or boardroom, is the prime directive.

We are told by authorities it is in our nature to be so aggressive, belligerent, and selfish and our past not only reveals that but has further conditioned us to exacerbate these traits. That being the case, more of the same is not only to be expected but openly encouraged. As such, our collective history is hijacked and revised to portray humanity's ascension in terms of conquests, enslavement, personal wealth, and warfare, and merely part of the natural Darwinian order of life. That mindset, in itself, creates a template and pattern of depletion that will consume itself and all that is a part of it.

There is another way. Critics may call it stepping backwards when teetering on the precipice, but much of what was discovered by the First Australians so long ago does not need to be relegated to ancient history; it can be seen as a guide map to tomorrow's salvation. Before countering with snide critiques regarding the so-called "impracticalities" of embracing the attitudes and values of the distant past, the skeptics should look to the example of Bolivia. The government has set off on a road rarely traveled through the legislation of what they refer to as the "Law of Mother Earth."[1] All mineral deposits and natural resources are now officially referred to as "sacred gifts."[2] Bolivia has been heavily criticized by the US and Britain in the UN talks for demanding steep carbon emission cuts, will establish eleven new rights for nature. Within these amendments is enshrined the protection of nature in that "all Bolivians will live in equilibrium and harmony with Mother Earth."[3]

This decision is extremely radical as "human activities should archive a dynamic balance with the cycles and processes inherent in Mother Earth."[4] This legislature, in tune with the Dreaming, states that humans are considered equal to all other entities. As it was in the Dreaming, the interrelationship between all participants in the web of creation is acknowledged as the fundamental truth upon which all forms of life are based.

Relying on Mother Earth for inspiration and guidance, thus reverting back to the ancient Indigenous Ways, the world can be saved. As the Kyoto Accord unravels by the day, and advanced nations quibble over potential incomes lost and who will take the first step, there doesn't seem to be much hope when the leaders and economic systems of today can do nothing except get in the way. But the Bolivians realize the teachings of long past, and the ancient values espoused offer another solution and alternative where Mother Earth stands unchallenged as the first priority.

As much as the advocates of the capitalist system that underpins the fabric of the global economy have dismissed these ancient ways as impractical and naïve, many captives of the system they champion are no longer listening. This book, and those that came before, is dedicated to any discerning individual who feels our governments are merely accountancy firms whose primary goal is to balance the books. The soul yearns for more, and we hope this book may offer some possibilities and perspectives that may go some way towards filling that vacuum.

In closing, we would like to conclude with one absolute: that whatever truth this book holds, it exists by virtue of its ability to reflect the spirit of the Dreaming. The content of *Out of Australia*, like all of our work, strives to remain in harmony with and promote a world view which is that of the Original Australians and has prevailed from at least the earliest times of *Homo sapiens* to the present day. A worldview which has sustained its people for such a phenomenal stretch of time and can speak to others outside that culture, like ourselves, so powerfully, has stood the test of time in a most impressive manner. For the sake of the earth and the generations that follow, it's time for everyone to start listening to that source. Tomorrow may be too late.

Finis

NOTES

1. Colin Simpson, *Adam in Ochre: Inside Aboriginal Australia* (Sydney, New South Wales: Angus & Robertson, 1956). Inside cover.

INTRODUCTION

1. Ronald Malcolm Gibbs, *The Aborigines* (Hawthorn, Australia: Longman Australia Pty Limited, 1975). 67.
2. Steven Strong and Evan Strong, *Constructing a New World Map*, 1st ed. (Lanham, MD: University Press of America Inc., 2008); ———, *Mary Magdalene's Dreaming: A Comparison of Aboriginal Wisdom and Gnostic Scripture* (Lanham, MD: University Press of America, Inc., 2008); ———, *Forgotten Origin* (Lanham, Md.: University Press of America, Inc., 2010).
3. Strong and Strong, *Forgotten Origin*. Back Cover: Burri
4. Allan C. Wilson and Rebecca L. Cann, "The Recent African Genesis of Humans: Genetic Studies Reveal That an African Woman of 200,000 Years Ago Was Our Common Ancestor," *Scientific American* 266, no. 4 (April 1992). 68.
5. Mike Morwood and Penny Van Oosterzee, *The Discovery of the Hobbit* (Milsons Point, Australia: Random House Australia Pty Ltd, 2007).
6. Josephine Flood, *Archaeology of the Dreamtime: The Story of Prehistoric Australia and Its People*, 6th ed. (Marleston, Australia: J.B. Publishing, 2004). 70.
7. Ibid. 69.
8. Jacqui Hayes, "Ancient Odyssey," *Cosmos* 2010. 42.
9. Hugh Rule and Stuart Goodman, *Gulpilil's Stories of the Dreamtime*, 3rd ed. (Sydney, Australia: William Collins Publishers Pty Limited, 1987). 11.
10. Flood, *Archaeology of the Dreamtime*. 171.
11. Paul Harrison, "The Gnostics—Releasing the Light Within," *Scientific Pantheism* (6 Mar. 1997), *www.pantheism.net/paul/gnostic.htm*. *Gospel of Eve (Epiphanius, Panarion 26.9.1)*.

CHAPTER 1: THE "FIRST RACE"

1. Willay Bitjar, 2012. Personal Communication to Steven Strong and Martin Yates.
2. Ibid. 3 (n).
3. Ibid.
4. Anne Wilson Schaef, *Native Wisdom for White Minds: Daily Reflections Inspired by the Native Peoples of the World* (Milsons Point, Australia: Random House Australia Pty Ltd, 1995).
5. Wilson and Cann, "The Recent African Genesis of Humans." 68.
6. Ibid. 72.
7. Ibid. 68.
8. Ibid.
9. John Gribbon and Jeremy Cherfas, *The Monkey Puzzle* (London: Bodley Head Ltd, 1982). In Robert Lawlor, *Voices of the First Day: Awakening in the Aboriginal Dreamtime* (Rochester, VT: Inner Traditions International, Ltd., 1991). 26
10. Gribbon and Cherfas, *The Monkey Puzzle*. In Lawlor, *Voices of the First Day*.
11. Lawlor, *Voices of the First Day*. 26
12. Ibid.
13. Gribbon and Cherfas, *The Monkey Puzzle*. 258. In Lawlor, *Voices of the First Day*. 26.
14. Leigh Dayton, "DNA Clue to Man's Origin: How Mungo Man Has Shaken the Human Family Tree," *The Australian*, 9 January 2001. 1 (n).
15. Hayes, "Ancient Odyssey." 42.
16. Ibid. 39.
17. Ibid. 40.
18. Ibid. Front Cover.
19. Ibid. 45.
20. Ibid.
21. Strong and Strong, *Constructing a New World Map*. 42.
22. Martin (producer/ reporter) Redfern and Pauline Newman, (producer), "Oldest American Footprints," in *The Science Show*, ed. Robyn Williams, (presenter) (Australia: A.B.C. Radio National, *www.abc.net.au/radio national/programs/scienceshow/oldest-american-footprints/3310064*, 11 Feb. 2006).
23. Strong and Strong, *Constructing a New World Map*. 48.
24. Redfern and Newman, "Oldest American Footprints."
25. Ibid.

26. Strong and Strong, *Constructing a New World Map*. 49.

27. Christopher Hardaker, *The First American: The Suppressed Story of the People Who Discovered the New World* (Franklin Lakes, N.J.: The Career Press Inc. (New Page Books, 2007). 187.

28. Ibid. 45.

29. Redfern and Newman, "Oldest American Footprints."

30. Walter A. Neves and Mark Hubbe, "Cranial Morphology of Early Americans from Lagoa Santa, Brazil: Implicatons for the Settlement of the New World," *Proceedings of the National Academy of Sciences of the United States of America* 102, no. 51 (2005), *https://www.ncbi.nlm.nih.gov/pmc/articles/PMC1317934/.*

31. Ibid.

32. Ibid.

33. Michael Winkler, "Rock Star of the Kimberley," *The Age* (20 Sept. 2004), *theage.com.au.*

34. Strong and Strong, *Constructing a New World Map*. 47.

35. *"First Americans Were Australian," BBC NEWS* (26 Aug.1999), *news.bbc .co.uk/2/hi/science/nature/430944.stm.*

36. Ibid.

37. Winkler, "Rock Star of the Kimberley."

38. Ibid.

39. Hugh Cairns and Bill Yidumbuma, *Dark Sparklers*, 2nd ed. (Merimbula, Australia: H.C. Cairnes, 2004). 42.

40. Ibid. 39.

41. Ibid. 42.

42. AAP, "First Australians Were Indian: Research," *Sydney Morning Herald*, 23 July 2009. (n).

43. Ibid.

44. Lawlor, *Voices of the First Day*. 120.

45. Strong and Strong, *Forgotten Origin*. 17.

46. Lawlor, *Voices of the First Day*. 120–121.

47. Bitjar.

CHAPTER 2: AN EXTENDED FAMILY

1. Flood, *Archaeology of the Dreamtime*. 3.

2. Ibid.

3. Ibid.

4. Ibid.

5. Ibid.

6. Dr Elena Govor, "The Barrinean Mystery," *My Dark Brother* (2000), *mydarkbrother.elena.id.au/Barrinean.htm.*

7. Ibid.

8. Ibid.

9. Brett Green and The Dhamurian Research Society, "The Little People," *Rainbow Spirit Warriors: Ka'bi Aboriginal Cultural Histories of S. E. Queensland, Australia* (2004), *www.warriors.egympie.com.au/littlepeople .html.*

10. Ibid.

11. Ibid.

12. Ibid.

13. Ibid.

14. Ibid.

15. Ibid.

16. Ibid.

17. Ibid.

18. Flood, *Archaeology of the Dreamtime.* 69.

19. Ibid.

20. Ibid.

21. Ibid.

22. Ibid.

23. Ibid. 70.

24. Ibid. 7.

25. Tressa Jamison, "The Australian Aboriginal People: Dating the Colonization of Australia,"(2004), *www.biology.iastate.edu/*

26. "A haplotype is a group of genes within an organism that was inherited together from a single parent . . . A haplotype can describe a pair of genes inherited together from one parent on one chromosome, or it can describe all of the genes on a chromosome that were inherited together from a single parent. This group of genes was inherited together because of genetic linkage, or the phenomenon by which genes that are close to each other on the same chromosome are often inherited together." *www.nature.com/scitable/definition/haplotype-haplotypes-142*, "Halotype / Haplotypes,"(2013).

27. Jamison, "The Australian Aboriginal People: Dating the Colonization of Australia."

28. Ibid.

29. Ibid.

30. Ibid.

31. Keith Windschuttle and Tim Gillin, "The Extinction of the Australian Pygmies," *Quadrant*, June 2002, *quadrant.org.au/blogs/history–wars/2002/06/the-extinction-of-the-australian-pygmies.*

32. Ibid.

33. Josephine Flood, *The Original Australians: Story of the Aboriginal People* (Crows Nest, Australia: Allen and Unwin, 2006). 175.

34. Ibid.

35. Ibid.

36. Ibid.

37. Windschuttle and Gillin, "The Extinction of the Australian Pygmies."

38. Flood, *The Original Australians: Story of the Aboriginal People*. 173.

39. Ibid. 176.

CHAPTER 3: ANCIENT ORIGINAL AUSTRALIANS IN AMERICA (A CLOSER LOOK)

1. Hayes, "Ancient Odyssey." Front Cover.

2. Ibid. 39.

3. Ibid.

4. Ibid. 47.

5. Winkler, "Rock Star of the Kimberley."

6. Ibid.

7. Hardaker, *The First American*. 186.

8. Ibid.15.

9. Ibid.

10. Ibid.

11. Ibid.

12. Ibid.

13. Ibid.

14. Ibid.

15. Ibid.

16. Ibid.

17. Ibid. 10.

18. Ibid.

19. Ibid.

20. Ibid.

21. Ibid. 18.

22. Ibid. 186.

23. Ibid.

24. Ibid.

25. Ibid. 161.
26. Ibid. 11.
27. Ibid. 187.
28. Ibid.
29. Ibid. 45.
30. Ibid. 210.
31. Ibid. 211.
32. Ibid.
33. Ibid. 186.
34. Redfern and Newman, "Oldest American Footprints."
35. Ibid.
36. Ibid.
37. Ibid.
38. Ibid.
39. Ibid.
40. Ibid.
41. Hardaker, *The First American*. 186.

CHAPTER 4: THE TOSS OF A COIN

1. Bitjar.
2. Ibid.
3. Lawlor, *Voices of the First Day*. Back cover.
4. Ibid.
5. Tom Whaddy, "The Frog Who Was King," in *Aboriginal Narratives and Poems of New South Wales*, ed. Roland Robinson (Sydney, Australia: Hale & Iremonger Pty Ltd, 1989). 61.
6. Ibid.
7. Ibid.
8. Ibid.
9. Ibid.
10. Ibid.
11. Ibid.
12. Ibid.
13. Ibid.
14. Ibid. 62.
15. Ibid.
16. Lawlor, *Voices of the First Day*. Back Cover.
17. Flood, *Archaeology of the Dreamtime*. 180.
18. Ibid. 2.
19. Ibid. 3.

20. Ibid.
21. Ibid. 115.
22. Flood, *The Original Australians: Story of the Aboriginal People*. 175.
23. Flood, *Archaeology of the Dreamtime*. 3.
24. Ibid. 2.
25. Winkler, "Rock Star of the Kimberley."
26. Ibid.
27. Ibid.
28. Andrew Carswell and Robert Cockburn, "Wurdi Youang Rocks Could Prove Aborigines Were First Astronomers,"(5 Feb 2011), *www.news.com.au/technology/sci-tech/ancient-aboriginal-eyes-were-on-the-skies/story-fn5fsgyc-1226000523978#ixzz1D9uDPgfE.*
29. Ibid. .
30. Ibid.
31. Ibid.
32. Ibid.
33. Ibid.
34. Ibid.
35. Ray P. Noris et al., "Wurdi Youang: An Australia Aboriginal Stone Arrangement with Possible Solar Indications," *Rock Art Research*, (28 Sept. 2012), *www.academia.edu/2064394/Wurdi_Youang_an_Australian_Aboriginal_stone_arrangement_with_possible_solar_indications*
36. Carswell and Cockburn, "Wurdi Youang Rocks Could Prove Aborigines Were First Astronomers."
37. Ibid.
38. Karno (Ramindjeri Elder) Walker, 2012.

CHAPTER 5: THE FIRST RELIGION

1. Harrison, "The Gnostics—Releasing the Light Within." *Gospel of Eve (Epiphanius, Panarion 26.9.1)*.
2. George W. MacRae, R. McL. Wilson, and Douglas M. Parrott, "The Gospel of Mary (Bg 8502,*1*)," in *The Nag Hammadi Library in English*, ed. James M. Robinson (New York: HarperSanFancisco, 1990). 525 (verse 10).
3. Ibid.
4. Ibid. 526 (verse 10).
5. G. R. S. Mead, *Pistis Sophia: The Gnostic Tradition of Mary Magdalene, Jesus and His Disciples*, trans. G. R. S. Mead, Dover ed. (Mineola, NY: Dover Publications Inc., 2005). 20.
6. Ibid. 100.

7. Wesley W. Isenberg, "The Gospel of Philip (Ii,*3*)," in *The Nag Hammadi Library in English*, ed. James M. Robinson (New York: HarperSanFrancisco, 1990). 148 (verse 63–64)

8. Ibid. (verse 64).

9. Ibid.

10. Marvin Meyer, *The Gospel of Thomas: The Hidden Sayings of Jesus*, trans. Marvin Meyer, 1st ed. (New York: HarperSanFrancisco, 1992). 33 (verse 21).

11. Ibid.

12. Stephen Emmel, trans., "The Dialogue of the Savior (Iii,*5*)," in *The Nag Hammadi Library in English*, ed. James M. Robinson (New York: HarperSanFrancisco, 1990). 253 (verse 83).

13. Mead, *Pistis Sophia*. 181.

14. Thomas O. Lambdin, trans., "The Gospel of Thomas (Ii,*2*)," in *The Nag Hammadi Library in English*, ed. James M. Robinson (New York: HarperSanFrancisco, 1990). 138 (verse 114).

15. Margaret Barker, "What Did King Josiah Reform?," *Glimpses of Lehi's Jerusalem* (2008), *mi.byu.edu/publications/books/?bookid=2&chapid=36*

16. Diane Bell, *Daughters of the Dreaming*, 3rd ed. (North Melbourne, Australia: Spinifex Press Pty Ltd, 2002). 223.

17. Simon Roach, "The Three Brothers Story as Told by Aunty Millie Boyd," *Byron Bay Echo*, 25 May 2005. 17 (n).

18. "The Dirahnggan Who Lived in a Cave," in *Aboriginal Stories from the North Coast*, ed. Norma Hawkins (The North Coast Institute of Aboriginal Community Education). 12–17.

19. Jacobus (Comp.) de Voragine and William Caxton (trans.), eds., *Here Followeth the Life of St. Mary Magdalene*, vol. 4 Medieval Sourcebook, Legenda Aurea (the Golden Legend or Lives of the Saints) *(http://sourcebooks.fordham.edu/halsall/basis/goldenlegend/GoldenLegend-Volume4.asp)*

20. Big Bill Neidjie, Stephen Davis, and Allan Fox, *Australia's Kakadu Man Bill Neidjie*, Revised ed. (Darwin, Australia: Resource Managers Pty Ltd, 1986). 58.

21. Harrison, "The Gnostics—Releasing the Light Within."

22. Neidjie, Davis, and Fox, *Australia's Kakadu Man Bill Neidjie*. 58.

23. Bill Neidjie, *Story About Feeling*, ed. Keith Taylor (Broome, Australia: Magabala Books, 1989). 19.

24. Sharon Rose, "Mary Magdalene, Apostle of Apostles," *New Dawn* Autumn/Winter, Special Issue 2 (2006).

25. Mead, *Pistis Sophia*. 27.

26. Ibid.

27. Ibid. 26–27.

28. Ibid. 27–28.

29. Ibid. 28.

30. Alexander Wyclif Reed, *Aboriginal Myths, Legends & Fables* (Chatswood, Australia: Reed Part of William Heinemann Australia, 1993; reprint, 1993). 20.

31. "Genesis," in *Holy Bible*. (2:7)

32. Ibid. (1:29).

33. Reed, *Aboriginal Myths, Legends & Fables*. 20.

34. Ibid. 21.

35. William Jenkyn Thomas, "A Legend of the Great Flood," in *Some Myths and Legends of the Australian Aborigines, www.sacred-texts.com/aus/mla/mla09.htm* (2003) (Melbourne, Australia: Whitcombin and Tombs Ltd, 1923).

36. Ibid.

37. Ibid.

38. Reed, *Aboriginal Myths, Legends & Fables*. 97.

39. George W. MacRae, trans. and Douglas M. Parrott ed., "The Apocalypse of Adam (V,5)," in *The Nag Hammadi Library in English*, ed. James M. Robinson (New York: HarperSanFrancisco, 1990). 279 (verse 64).

40. Ibid.

41. Roland Eggleston, *How the Sea Got Its Fish, When Yondi Pushed up the Sky* (Sydney, Australia: Australian Publishing Company, 1964). 19.

42. Ibid.

43. Ibid. 21.

44. MacRae and Parrott ed., "The Nag Hammadi Library." 279 (verse 64).

CHAPTER 6: PYRAMIDS ACROSS THE WATERS

1. Chris Boyd, "Historic Importance of Orion/Taurus Sky Region to the Ancients,"(28 Feb. 2009), *www.articlesbase.com/history-articles/historic-importance-of-oriontaurus-sky-region-to-the-ancients-794596.html*.

2. Ibid.

3. Treasure Enterprises Australia, "Australia's Unexplained Mysteries and Enigmas," *www.treasureenterprises.com/Miscellaneous/Archaeology_in_australia.htm*.

4. Ibid.

5. Ibid.

6. Robin Strummer, "Brit Brains Solve the Riddle of the 'Rang," *The Independant* (23 March 1997), *www.independant.co.uk/news/brit-brains-solve-the-riddle-of-the-rang-1274522.html*.

7. Ellie Crystal, "Australia—Egypt Connection," *www.crystalinks.com/egyptaustralia2.html.*

8. Michael Terry, "Australia's Unwritten History," *Walkabout* August (1967). 21 "[i]n February 1964 the tomb of a woman, probably dating back to 1,000 B.C., was found on the site of an ancient city in the Jordan Valley. Examination of the body suggested that eucalyptus oil had been used to embalm it. The only sources then of such oil were the gum-trees of Australia and New Guinea. Now, of course, they are relatively common overseas but only since Baron von Mueller instituted a seed exchange between Australia and other parts of the world . . ."

9. Tristan Rankine, "Hidden Bits of History: Awareness Quest," (2011), *www.awarenessquest.com/AAA/research.htm.*

10. Ibid.

11. Ibid.

12. Strong and Strong, *Constructing a New World Map.* 112.

13. Ibid.

14. Ibid.

15. Crystal, "Australia—Egypt Connection."

16. Ibid.

17. Rankine, "Hidden Bits of History: Awareness Quest."

18. Ibid.

19. Ibid.

20. Strong and Strong, *Constructing a New World Map.* 109.

21. Paul Kelly, Kev Carmody, and The Messengers, "From Little Things Big Things Grow," in *Comedy* (Australia 1991).

22. Raymond Johnson and Edith May Rumbel, *Kariong Glyphs* (1997). 1.

23. Dr R.M. de Jonge, "Burial Site of Lord Nefer-Ti-Ru: Son of King Khufu, C.2637–2614 Fourth Dynasty of Egypt," *Egyptians in Australia,* *www.slideshare.net/rmdejonge/go-sford-4.*

24. Ibid.

25. Ibid.

26. Ibid.

27. Johnson and Rumbel, *Kariong Glyphs.* 2.

28. de Jonge, "Burial Site of Lord Nefer-Ti-Ru: Son of King Khufu, C.2637–2614 BC, Fourth Dynasty of Egypt."

29. Johnson and Rumbel, *Kariong Glyphs.* 3.

30. Raymond Johnson and Edith May Rumbel, *Basic Hieroglypica* (1997). 94, no. 2886.

31. Ibid. 50, no. 1559.

32. Ibid. 48, no. 1499.

33. Johnson and Rumbel, *Kariong Glyphs*. 1.
34. Doug MacPherson, 1980. Personal Communication from Elder Lyle Roberts.
35. "The Gympie Pryamid: Calculations," *www.gympiepyramid.org/calc.html.*
36. Greg Jeffreys, "Gympie Pyramid Investigation Dig " in *The Big Dig Report http://www.gympiepyramid.org.*
37. Ibid.
38. Ibid.
39. Dhamurian Society, "The Gympie Pyramid: The Mysterious 'Slag,'" *www.gympie.org/slag.html.*
40. Boyd, "Historic Importance of Orion/Taurus Sky Region to the Ancients."
41. Ibid.
42. Ibid.
43. Ibid.
44. Ibid.
45. Lawlor, *Voices of the First Day*. 75.

CHAPTER 7: DOGON DREAMING

1. Shannon Dorey, "The Dreamtime & the Dogon: Records of Encounters with Our Alien Creators," *New Dawn* Spring, Special Issue #13 (2010). 14.
2. Ibid. 11.
3. Ibid.
4. John McGrath, 2011. Personal Communication.
5. Ibid.
6. Dorey, "The Dreamtime & the Dogon: Records of Encounters with Our Alien Creators." 11.
7. Ibid. 16.
8. Cairns and Yidumbuma, *Dark Sparklers*. 42.
9. Ibid.
10. Ibid.
11. Dorey, "The Dreamtime & the Dogon: Records of Encounters with Our Alien Creators." 11.
12. Ibid.
13. Ibid.
14. Ibid.
15. Ibid.
16. Ibid. 12.
17. Ibid.

18. Ibid.
19. Ibid.
20. Ibid.
21. Ibid. 13.
22. Ibid.
23. Ibid. 11.
24. Ibid.
25. Ibid. 13.
26. Ibid.
27. Flood, *Archaeology of the Dreamtime*. 171.
28. Ibid.
29. Ibid.
30. Dorey, "The Dreamtime & the Dogon: Records of Encounters with Our Alien Creators." 15.
31. Ibid.
32. Ibid.
33. Ibid.
34. Ibid. 11.
35. Ibid. 14.
36. Ibid.
37. Ibid. 16.
38. Ibid. 14.
39. Ibid.
40. Ibid.
41. Flood, *Archaeology of the Dreamtime*. 169.
42. Winkler, "Rock Star of the Kimberley."
43. Ibid.
44. Josephine Flood, *Rock Art of the Dreamtime: Images of Ancient Australia* (Sydney, Australia: Angus and Robertson, 1997). 294.
45. Dorey, "The Dreamtime & the Dogon: Records of Encounters with Our Alien Creators." 16.
46. Ibid.
47. Ibid.
48. Ibid.
49. Ibid.
50. Ibid.
51. Ibid. 11.
52. Alan Baker, *Sirius—the Mysteries of the Dog Star, The Enigmas of History: Myths, Mysteries and Madness from around the World* (Edinburgh, UK: Mainstream Publishing Company, 2008). 31–39.

53. Ibid. 35.
54. Ibid.
55. Ibid.
56. Ibid.
57. Ibid. 31.
58. Ibid.
59. Ibid. 35.
60. Ibid. 35.
61. Dorey, "The Dreamtime & the Dogon: Records of Encounters with Our Alien Creators." 11.
62. Baker, *Sirius—the Mysteries of the Dog Star*. 32.
63. McGrath.
64. Ibid.
65. Ibid.
66. Ibid.
67. Ibid.
68. Ibid.
69. Lawlor, *Voices of the First Day*. 26.
70. Dorey, "The Dreamtime & the Dogon: Records of Encounters with Our Alien Creators." 11.
71. Ibid.
72. Winkler, "Rock Star of the Kimberley."
73. Ibid.

CHAPTER 8: THE FIRST RELIGION (PART 2)

1. MacRae, Wilson, and Parrott, "Nag Hammadi Library." 525, (verse 10).
2. Ibid.
3. Hermann Klaatsch, *The Evolution and Progress of Mankind*, ed. Adolf Heilborn and Joseph McCabe (Translator) (New York: Frederick A. Stokes Company Publishers, 1923). 227.
4. Ibid.
5. Jean Doresse, *The Secret Books of the Egyptian Gnostics: An Introduction to the Gnostic Coptic Manuscripts Discovered at Chenoboskion* (New York: MJF Books, Inner Traditions International, 1996). 44.
6. Ibid.
7. Ibid. 38.
8. Ibid. 38–39.
9. Ibid. 261.
10. Ibid. 2.

11. Graham Hancock, *Fingerprints of the Gods: A Quest for the Beginning and the End* (London: Mandarin Paperbacks, 1996). 112.

12. Ibid.

13. Meyer, *The Gospel of Thomas*. 59 (verse 95).

14. Ibid. 25 (verse 6).

15. Mead, *Pistis Sophia*. 20 (chap.17).

16. Ibid.

17. Ibid.

CHAPTER 9: A NATION OF ADAMS AND EVES

1. Kevin Butler, Kate Cameron, and Bob Percival, *The Myth of Terra Nullius: Invasion and Resistance—the Early Years* (North Sydney: Board of Studies NSW, 1995). 4.

2. Adolphus Peter Elkin, *Aboriginal Men of High Degree* (Rochester, Vermont / St Lucia, QLD: Inner Traditions International / University of Queensland Press, 1994). 150.

3. Ibid.

4. Ibid.

5. Ibid. 151.

6. Ibid.

7. "Towards the Light," *BBC Today* (18th Sept. 2008), *news.bbc.co.uk/today/hi/today/newsid_7622000/7622456.stm*.

8. Ibid.

9. Jane Dreaper, "Study into Near-Death Experiences," *BBC News* (18 Sept. 2008), *news.bbc.co.uk/2/mobile/health/7621608.stm*.

10. "Towards the Light."

11. Elkin, *Aboriginal Men of High Degree*. 151.

12. Ibid. 153.

13. Ibid. 142.

14. Ibid. 143.

15. Ibid. 147.

16. Ibid. 144.

17. Lawlor, *Voices of the First Day*. 358

18. Elkin, *Aboriginal Men of High Degree*. 142.

19. Ibid.

20. Ibid.

21. Ibid. 152.

22. James Keith Elliott, "The 'Secret' Gospel of Mark," in *The Apocryphal New Testament: A Collection of Apocryphal Christian Literature in an English*

Translation Based on M. R. James (Oxford, UK: Oxford University Press, 2007). 149.

23. Ibid.
24. Ibid.
25. Ibid.
26. Ibid.
27. "The Gospel According to John," in *The Bible*. (11:16).

CHAPTER 10: MYSTICS OR MORONS?

1. Lawlor, *Voices of the First Day*. 79.
2. Nigel Parbury, *Survival* (Sydney, Australia: Ministry of Aboriginal Affairs, 1991). 67.
3. Ibid.
4. Lawlor, *Voices of the First Day*. 79.
5. Flood, *Archaeology of the Dreamtime*. 95.
6. Lawlor, *Voices of the First Day*. 79.
7. Flood, *Archaeology of the Dreamtime*. 199.
8. Ibid.
9. Ibid. 200–201.
10. Ibid. 207.
11. Ibid.
12. Eggleston, *How the Sea Got Its Fish*. 19–21.
13. Lawlor, *Voices of the First Day*.83.
14. Ibid.
15. Ibid. 86.
16. Ibid.
17. Ibid. 200.
18. Ibid. 206.
19. Ibid. 201.
20. Gibbs, *The Aborigines*. 11.
21. Lawlor, *Voices of the First Day*. 78.
22. Ibid.
23. Parbury, *Survival*. 66.
24. Ibid.
25. Ibid. 67.
26. Flood, *Rock Art of the Dreamtime*. 229.
27. Ibid. 222.
28. Ibid. 123.
29. Ibid. 221.
30. Lawlor, *Voices of the First Day*. 85.

31. Flood, *Rock Art of the Dreamtime*. 1.
32. Flood, *Archaeology of the Dreamtime*. 210–211.
33. Ibid. 86.

CHAPTER 11: THE SHIP'S CARGO

1. Donald F. Thomson, "The Aborigines of Australia," in *Australia Junior Encyclopedia*, ed. Charles Barrett (Melbourne, Australia: The Australian Educational Foundation, 1958). 70.
2. Ibid.
3. Ibid.
4. Butler, Cameron, and Percival, *The Myth of Terra Nullius: Invasion and Resistance—the Early Years*. 34.
5. "400 Year Old Aboriginal Skull," *The Daily Telegraph*, 8 Sept 2004.
6. Ibid.
7. Ibid.
8. Isabel McBryde, *Aboriginal Prehistory in New England* (Sydney, Australia: Sydney University Press, 1974). 343.
9. Ibid.
10. Ibid.
11. Ibid. 344.
12. Ibid. 343–344.
13. Ibid. 344.
14. Ibid. 143.
15. Ibid.
16. Ibid. 344.
17. Ibid. 344.
18. Ibid. 343–344.
19. Ibid. 343.
20. Katherine Hibbert, "Bigfoot's 20,000–Year-Old Walkabout," *The Sunday Times* (30th April 2006), *www.thesundaytimes.co.uk/sto/style/article 199761.ece*.
21. Ibid.
22. Ibid.
23. Ibid.
24. Ibid.
25. Ibid.
26. Ibid.
27. Flood, *Archaeology of the Dreamtime*. 45.
28. Ibid.
29. Ibid.

30. Ibid.

31. Ibid.

32. Michael W. Ryan, *White Man, Black Man* (Milton, Queensland: The Jacaranda Press Pty Ltd, 1969). 21.

33. Ibid.

34. Ibid. 46.

35. Jane E. Harrison, "The Kouretes and Zeus Kouros: A Study in Pre-Historic Sociology," *The Annual of the British School at Athens,* Vol. 15 (Athens: British School at Athens, 1908/1909). 308–338.

36. Mircea Eliade, *Rites and Symbols of Initiation: The Mysteries of Birth and Rebirth*, (New York: Harper Colophon Books, 1958). 83.

37. Ibid, 111.

38. Jennifer Hoff, *Bundajalung Jugun Bundjalung Country* (Lismore, New South Wales: Richmond River Historical Society Inc., 2006). 2.

39. Ibid.

40. Hermann Klaatsch, *Some Notes on Scientific Travel Amongst the Black Populatioms of Tropical Australia in 1904, 1905, 1906* (Adelaide: Australasian Association for the Advancement of Science, 1907). 9.

41. Ibid.

42. Ibid.

CHAPTER 12: THE ORIGINS OF THE 4 R'S (READIN', 'RITIN', 'RITHMETIC, AND 'RT)

1. Klaatsch, *The Evolution and Progress of Mankind.* 2

2. Flood, *Archaeology of the Dreamtime.* 180.

3. Flood, *Rock Art of the Dreamtime.* 178.

4. Flood, *Archaeology of the Dreamtime.* 166.

5. Ibid. 44.

6. Klaatsch, *The Evolution and Progress of Mankind.* 136.

7. Ibid.

8. Ibid. 137.

9. Ibid.

10. Rankine, "Hidden Bits of History: Awareness Quest."

11. Lawlor, *Voices of the First Day.* 120.

12. Ibid.

13. Carswell and Cockburn, "Wurdi Youang Rocks Could Prove Aborigines Were First Astronomers."

14. Ibid.

15. Ibid.

16. Ibid.

17. Ibid.
18. Klaatsch, *The Evolution and Progress of Mankind.* 137.
19. Ibid.
20. Lawlor, *Voices of the First Day.* Back Cover.

CHAPTER 13: THE MYTH OF TERRA NULLIUS

1. Butler, Cameron, and Percival, *The Myth of Terra Nullius: Invasion and Resistance—the Early Years.* 39.
2. Ibid. 5.
3. Ibid. 5.
4. Ibid. 31.
5. Ibid. 36.
6. Ibid.
7. Ibid.
8. Ibid.
9. Ibid. 37.
10. Ibid. 43.
11. Ibid. 44.
12. Ibid.
13. Ibid.
14. Ibid.
15. Ibid. 46.
16. Ibid. 39.
17. Ibid. 39.
18. Ibid. 48.
19. Ibid. 49.
20. Ibid. 51.
21. Ibid. 50.
22. Ibid. 50.
23. Ibid. 52.
24. Ibid.
25. Ibid.
26. Ibid.
27. Ibid.
28. Ibid.
29. Ibid.
30. Ibid. 49.
31. Ibid.
32. Ibid.
33. Ibid. 49.

34. Ibid.
35. Ibid.
36. Ibid.
37. Ibid.
38. Ibid. 50.
39. Ibid.
40. Ibid. 50–51.
41. Ibid. 50.
42. Ibid. 51.
43. Ibid.
44. Ibid.
45. Ibid. 52.
46. Ibid. 53.
47. Ibid.
48. Ibid. 71.
49. Ibid.
50. Ibid.
51. Ibid.
52. Ibid.
53. Ibid.
54. Ibid. 84.
55. Ibid.
56. Ibid. 90.
57. Eric Willmot, *Pemulwuy: The Rainbow Warrior* (Sydney, Australia: Bantam Books, 1994).

CONCLUSION

1. Positive News, "Law of Mother Earth Approved in Bolivia," Positive News Publishing Ltd, *positivenews.org.uk/2012/environment/9982/law-mother-earth-approved-bolivia/*.
2. Ibid.
3. Ibid.
4. Rene Oscar Martinez (President Chamber of Senators) Callahuanca, "Law of Mother Earth: The Rights of Our Planet, a Vision from Bolivia," World Future Fund, *www.worldfuturefund.org/Projects/Indicators/motherearthbolivia.html*. Chapter. 1 Objects and Principles, Article 2, No. 1.

BIBLIOGRAPHY

"400 Year Old Aboriginal Skull." *The Daily Telegraph*, 8th Sept 2004.

AAP. "First Australians Were Indian: Research." *Sydney Morning Herald*, 23 July 2009, (N).

Australia, Treasure Enterprises. "Australia's Unexplained Mysteries and Enigmas." www.treasureenterprises.com/Miscellaneous/Archaeology_in_australia.htm.

Baker, Alan. *Sirius—the Mysteries of the Dog Star, The Enigmas of History: Myths, Mysteries and Madness from around the World*. Edinburgh, UK: Mainstream Publishing Company, 2008.

Barker, Margaret. "What Did King Josiah Reform?" *Glimpses of Lehi's Jerusalem* (2008), http://mi.byu.edu/publications/books/?bookid=2&chapid=36.

Bell, Diane. *Daughters of the Dreaming*. 3rd ed. North Melbourne, Australia: Spinifex Press Pty Ltd, 2002.

Bitjar, Willay. 2012.

Boyd, Chris. "Historic Importance of Orion/Taurus Sky Region to the Ancients." (28 Feb. 2009), www.articlesbase.com/history-articles/historic-importance-of-oriontaurus-sky-region-to-the-ancients-794596.html.

Butler, Kevin, Kate Cameron, and Bob Percival. *The Myth of Terra Nullius: Invasion and Resistance—the Early Years*. North Sydney: Board of Studies NSW, 1995.

Cairns, Hugh, and Bill Yidumbuma. *Dark Sparklers*. 2nd ed. Merimbula, Australia: H.C. Cairnes, 2004.

Callahuanca, Rene Oscar Martinez (President Chamber of Senators). "Law of Mother Earth: The Rights of Our Planet, a Vision from Bolivia." World Future Fund, www.worldfuturefund.org/Projects/Indicators/motherearth bolivia.html.

Carswell, Andrew, and Robert Cockburn. "Wurdi Youang Rocks Could Prove Aborigines Were First Astronomers." (5 Feb. 2011), www.news.com.au/technology/sci-tech/ancient-aboriginal-eyes-were-on-the-skies/story-fn5fsgyc-1226000523978#ixzz1D9uDPgfE.

Crystal, Ellie. "Australia—Egypt Connection." http://www.crystalinks.com/egyptaustralia2.html.

Dayton, Leigh. "DNA Clue to Man's Origin: How Mungo Man Has Shaken the Human Family Tree." *The Australian*, 9 January 2001.

de Jonge, Dr. R.M. "Burial Site of Lord Nefer-Ti-Ru: Son of King Khufu, C.2637–2614 BC, Fourth Dynasty of Egypt." *Egyptians in Australia*, www.slideshare.net/rmdejonge/go-sford-4.

de Voragine, Jacobus (Comp.), and William Caxton (trans.), eds. *Here Followeth the Life of St. Mary Magdalene*. Edited by F. S. Ellis (Temple Classics ed.) 1900. Vol. 4. Medieval Sourcebook, Legenda Aurea (the Golden Legend or Lives of the Saints): http://sourcebooks.fordham.edu/halsall/basis/goldenlegend/GoldenLegend-Volume4.asp, 2001.

Dhamurian Society. "The Gympie Pyramid: The Mysterious 'Slag.'" http://www.gympie.org/slag.html.

"The Dirahnggan Who Lived in a Cave." In *Aboriginal Stories from the North Coast*, edited by Norma Hawkins: The North Coast Institute of Aboriginal Community Education.

Doresse, Jean. *The Secret Books of the Egyptian Gnostics: An Introduction to the Gnostic Coptic Manuscripts Discovered at Chenoboskion*. New York, N.Y.: MJF Books, Inner Traditions International, 1996.

Dorey, Shannon. "The Dreamtime & the Dogon: Records of Encounters with Our Alien Creators." *New Dawn* Spring, Special Issue #13 (2010).

Dreaper, Jane. "Study into Near Death Experiences." *BBC News* (18 Sept. 2008), news.bbc.co.uk/2/mobile/health/7621608.stm.

Eggleston, Roland. *How the Sea Got Its Fish, When Yondi Pushed up the Sky*. Sydney, Australia: Australian Publishing Company, 1964.

Eliade, Mircea. *Rites and Symbols of Initiation: The Mysteries of Birth and Rebirth*, (New York: Harper Colophon Books, 1958).

Elkin, Adolphus Peter. *Aboriginal Men of High Degree*. Rochester, Vermont / St Lucia, QLD: Inner Traditions International / University of Queensland Press, 1994.

Elliott, James Keith. "The 'Secret' Gospel of Mark." In *The Apocryphal New Testament: A Collection of Apocryphal Christian Literature in an English Translation Based on M. R. James*, Pp. 148–49. Oxford, UK: Oxford University Press, 2007.

Emmel, Stephen, trans. "The Dialogue of the Savior (Iii,5)." In *The Nag Hammadi Library in English*, edited by James M. Robinson, Pp. 246–55. New York: HarperSanFrancisco, 1990.

"First Americans Were Australian." *BBC NEWS* (26 Aug. 1999), news.bbc.co.uk/2/hi/science/nature/430944.stm.

Flood, Josephine. *Archaeology of the Dreamtime: The Story of Prehistoric Australia and Its People.* 6th ed. Marleston, Australia: J.B. Publishing, 2004.

———. *The Original Australians: Story of the Aboriginal People.* Crows Nest, Australia: Allen and Unwin, 2006.

———. *Rock Art of the Dreamtime: Images of Ancient Australia.* Sydney, Australia: Angus and Robertson, 1997.

"Genesis." In *Holy Bible.*

Gibbs, Ronald Malcolm. *The Aborigines.* Hawthorn, Australia: Longman Australia Pty Limited, 1975.

"The Gospel According to John." In *The Bible.*

Govor, Dr Elena. "The Barrinean Mystery." *My Dark Brother* (2000), http://mydarkbrother.elena.id.au/Barrinean.htm

Green, Brett, and The Dhamurian Research Society. "The Little People." *Rainbow Spirit Warriors: Ka'bi Aboriginal Cultural Histories of S. E. Queensland, Australia* (2004), www.warriors.egympie.com.au/littlepeople.html.

Gribbon, John, and Jeremy Cherfas. *The Monkey Puzzle.* London: Bodley Head Ltd, 1982.

"The Gympie Pyramid: Calculations." http://www.gympiepyramid.org/calc.html.

Hancock, Graham. *Fingerprints of the Gods: A Quest for the Beginning and the End.* London: Mandarin Paperbacks, 1996.

Hardaker, Christopher. *The First American: The Suppressed Story of the People Who Discovered the New World.* Franklin Lakes, NJ: The Career Press Inc. (New Page Books), 2007.

Harrison, Jane E. "The Kouretes and Zeus Kouros: A Study in Pre-Historic Sociology," *The Annual of the British School at Athens,* Vol. 15. Athens: British School at Athens, 1908/1909, 308–338.

Harrison, Paul. "The Gnostics—Releasing the Light Within." *Scientific Pantheism* (6 Mar. 1997), www.pantheism.net/paul/gnostic.htm.

Hayes, Jacqui. "Ancient Odyssey." *Cosmos,* 2010, 39–47.

Hibbert, Katherine. "Bigfoot's 20,000–Year-Old Walkabout." *The Sunday Times* (30th April 2006), www.thesundaytimes.co.uk/sto/style/article199761.ece.

Hoff, Jennifer. *Bundajalung Jugun Bundjalung Country.* Lismore, New South Wales: Richmond River Historical Society Inc., 2006.

www.nature.com/scitable/definition/haplotype-haplotypes-142. "Halotype / Haplotypes." (2013).

Isenberg, Wesley W. "The Gospel of Philip (Ii,3)." In *The Nag Hammadi Library in English,* edited by James M. Robinson, Pp. 141–60. New York: HarperSanFrancisco, 1990.

Jamison, Tressa. "The Australian Aboriginal People: Dating the Colonization of Australia." (2004), http://www.biology.iastate.edu/International-
Trips/1Australia/04papers/TressaAborigOrign.htm.

Jeffreys, Greg. "Gympie Pyramid Investigation Dig " *In The Big Dig Report:*
http://www.gympiepyramid.org, 2007.

Johnson, Raymond, and Edith May Rumbel. *Basic Hieroglypica* 1997.

———. *Kariong Glyphs* 1997.

Kelly, Paul, Kev Carmody, and The Messengers. "From Little Things Big
Things Grow." In *Comedy*. Australia, 1991.

Klaatsch, Hermann. *Some Notes on Scientific Travel Amongst the Black Populatioms of Tropical Australia in 1904, 1905, 1906*, 1–16. Adelaide: Australasian
Association for the Advancement of Science, 1907.

———. *The Evolution and Progress of Mankind.* Edited by Adolf Heilborn and
Joseph McCabe (Translator). New York: Frederick A. Stokes Company
Publishers, 1923.

Lambdin, Thomas O., trans. "The Gospel of Thomas (Ii,2)." In *The Nag Hammadi Library in English*, edited by James M. Robinson, Pp.126–38. New
York: HarperSanFrancisco, 1990.

Lawlor, Robert. *Voices of the First Day: Awakening in the Aboriginal Dreamtime.*
Rochester, VT: Inner Traditions International, Ltd., 1991.

McGrath, John. 2011.

MacPherson, Doug. 1980.

MacRae, George W., trans., and Douglas M. Parrott, ed. "The Apocalypse of
Adam (V,5)." In *The Nag Hammadi Library in English*, edited by James M.
Robinson, Pp. 279–86. New York, N.Y.: HarperSanFrancisco, 1990.

MacRae, George W., R. McL. Wilson, and Douglas M. Parrott. "The Gospel
of Mary (Bg 8502,1)." In *The Nag Hammadi Library in English*, edited by
James M. Robinson, Pp. 524–27. New York: HarperSanFancisco, 1990.

McBryde, Isabel. *Aboriginal Prehistory in New England*. Sydney, Australia: Sydney University Press, 1974.

Mead, G. R. S. *Pistis Sophia: The Gnostic Tradition of Mary Magdalene, Jesus and
His Disciples.* Translated by G. R. S. Mead. Dover ed. Mineola, NY: Dover
Publications Inc., 2005.

Meyer, Marvin. *The Gospel of Thomas: The Hidden Sayings of Jesus.* Translated by
Marvin Meyer. 1st ed. New York: HarperSanFrancisco, 1992.

Morwood, Mike, and Penny Van Oosterzee. *The Discovery of the Hobbit.* Milsons Point, Australia: Random House Australia Pty Ltd, 2007.

Neidjie, Big Bill, Stephen Davis, and Allan Fox. *Australia's Kakadu Man Bill
Neidjie.* Revised ed. Darwin, Australia: Resource Managers Pty Ltd, 1986.

Neidjie, Bill. *Story About Feeling*. Edited by Keith Taylor. Broome, Australia: Magabala Books, 1989.

Neves, Walter A., and Mark Hubbe. "Cranial Morphology of Early Americans from Lagoa Santa, Brazil: Implicatons for the Settlement of the New World." *Proceedings of the National Academy of Sciences of the United States of America* 102, no. 51 (2005), http://www.pubmedcentral.nih.gov/articlerender.fcgi?artid=1317934.

Noris, Ray P., Cilla Norris , Duane W. Hamacher, and Reg Abrahams. "Wurdi Youang: An Australia Aboriginal Stone Arrangement with Possible Solar Indications." *Rock Art Research*, 28 Sept. 2012.

Parbury, Nigel. *Survival*. Sydney, Australia: Ministry of Aboriginal Affairs, 1991.

Positive News. "Law of Mother Earth Approved in Bolivia." Positive News Publishing Ltd, positivenews.org.uk/2012/environment/9982/law-mother-earth-approved-bolivia/.

Rankine, Tristan. "Hidden Bits of History: Awareness Quest." (2011), www.awarenessquest.com/AAA/research.htm.

Redfern, Martin (producer/ reporter), and Pauline Newman, (producer). "Oldest American Footprints." In *The Science Show*, edited by Robyn Williams, (presenter), (Transcript). Australia: A.B.C. Radio National, www .abc.net.au/radionational/programs/scienceshow/oldest-american-foot prints/3310064, 11 Feb. 2006.

Reed, Alexander Wyclif. *Aboriginal Myths, Legends & Fables*. Chatswood, Australia: Reed Part of William Heinemann Australia, 1993. Reprint, 1993.

Roach, Simon. "The Three Brothers Story as Told by Aunty Millie Boyd." *Byron Bay Echo*, 25 May 2005.

Rose, Sharon. "Mary Magdalene, Apostle of Apostles." *New Dawn* Autumn/ Winter, Special Issue 2 (2006).

Rule, Hugh, and Stuart Goodman. *Gulpilil's Stories of the Dreamtime*. 3rd ed. Sydney, Australia: William Collins Publishers Pty Limited, 1987.

Ryan, Michael W. *White Man, Black Man*. Milton, Queensland: The Jacaranda Press Pty Ltd, 1969.

Schaef, Anne Wilson. *Native Wisdom for White Minds: Daily Reflections Inspired by the Native Peoples of the World*. Milsons Point, Australia: Random House Australia Pty Ltd, 1995.

Simpson, Colin. *Adam in Ochre: Inside Aboriginal Australia*. Sydney, New South Wales: Angus & Robertson, 1956.

Strong, Steven, and Evan Strong. *Constructing a New World Map*. 1st ed. Lanham, MD: University Press of America Inc., 2008

————. *Forgotten Origin.* Lanham, MD: University Press of America, Inc., 2010.

————. *Mary Magdalene's Dreaming: A Comparison of Aboriginal Wisdom and Gnostic Scripture.* Lanham, MD: University Press of America, Inc., 2008.

Strummer, Robin. "Brit Brains Solve the Riddle of the 'Rang." *The Independant* (23 March 1997), http://www.independant.co.uk/news/brit-brains-solve-the-riddle-of-the-rang-1274522.html.

Terry, Michael. "Australia's Unwritten History." *Walkabout* August, (1967): 19–23.

Thomas, William Jenkyn. "A Legend of the Great Flood." In *Some Myths and Legends of the Australian Aborigines,* www.sacred-texts.com/aus/mla/mla09.htm (2003). Melbourne, Australia: Whitcombin and Tombs Ltd, 1923.

Thomson, Donald F. "The Aborigines of Australia." In *Australia Junior Encyclopedia,* edited by Charles Barrett, 70–97. Melbourne, Australia: The Australian Educational Foundation, 1958.

"Towards the Light." *BBC Today* (18th Sept. 2008), news.bbc.co.uk/today/hi/today/newsid_7622000/7622456.stm.

Walker, Karno (Ramindjeri Elder). 2012.

Whaddy, Tom. "The Frog Who Was King." In *Aboriginal Narratives and Poems of New South Wales,* edited by Roland Robinson. Sydney, Australia: Hale & Iremonger Pty Ltd, 1989.

Willmot, Eric. *Pemulwuy: The Rainbow Warrior.* Sydney, Australia: Bantam Books, 1994.

Wilson, Allan C., and Rebecca L. Cann. "The Recent African Genesis of Humans: Genetic Studies Reveal That an African Woman of 200,000 Years Ago Was Our Common Ancestor." *Scientific American* 266, no. 4 (April 1992): 68–73.

Windschuttle, Keith, and Tim Gillin. "The Extinction of the Australian Pygmies." *Quadrant* June 2002, www.quadrant.org.au/blogs/history-wars/2002/06/the-extinction-of-the-australian-pygmies.

Winkler, Michael. "Rock Star of the Kimberley." *The Age* (20 Sept. 2004), theage.com.au.

INDEX